Who's Using Your Tongue?

Vicki Smith Berdit

(formerly Vicki Smith White)

TRILOGY CHRISTIAN PUBLISHERS

TUSTIN, CA

TRILOGY

Trilogy Christian Publishers
A Wholly Owned Subsidary of Trinity Broadcasting Network
2442 Michelle Drive
Tustin, CA 92780

For information about special discounts for bulk purchases, please contact Trilogy Christian Publishing.

Trilogy Disclaimer: The views and content expressed in this book are those of the author and may not necessarily reflect the views and doctrine of Trilogy Christian Publishing or the Trinity Broadcasting Network.

Manufactured in the United States of America

10 9 8 7 6 5 4 3 2 1

Library of Congress Cataloging-in-Publication Data is available.

ISBN: 978-1-64773-271-4

E-ISBN: 978-1-64773-272-1

Contents

Dedication

This book is dedicated to the many faithful followers of Christ who honor Freedom's Way Ministries with their participation in our weekly teleconference teaching as well as weekday morning prayer and Bible reading. May God richly bless you through these pages with a deeper understanding and greater revelation of freedom from the deception of the enemy through a false tongue.

What shall be given unto thee? or what shall be done unto thee, thou false tongue?

Psalm 120:3

Foreword

When I initially received this manuscript in the mail, I saw the title, *Who's Using Your Tongue?* I was intrigued but a little bit hesitant. The reason was simple. Every Christian bookstore I have ever been in has a book on the shelf about the power of your tongue and that now-famous scripture about life and death in the words we use. I wondered what Vicki could write that we have not heard before. I knew the principles, and I have applied those principles in my life many times with great success. I know for a fact that they work.

At first, I set the book aside, thinking, *When I have time, I'll glance through it.* As it lay there on my desk, I would stare at it every day. To soothe my conscience, I moved it to the nightstand beside my bed, hoping to read some of it one night before going to sleep. Somehow, the spirit of God began to prompt me to start reading, and so I finally picked it up one night just as I was getting into bed.

I was only going to ease my conscience. Then, as I started reading, I found I was captivated by what is in this book! Vicki was writing about stuff we all know, but there was a fresh revelation and a fresh perspective I have not seen or heard before. After a while, I got out of bed, and hours later, I was still reading and praying the prayers in the book over my family and myself. This was revelation in a new perspective and truth that was setting me free in a whole new way. Finally, I went to bed and the next day made time to finish reading this book. I must admit that I prayed every prayer in every chapter, even if I didn't think I needed it.

Vicki has been a dear friend for years, and I highly recommend you read this book and apply the principles and the prayers she has penned down. She is a person that not only shares the principles God reveals to her, but also, I know, she applies them in ministry. She doesn't write about things that have not been tried and tested on the battlefield.

God has given her insight and strategies to bring down the enemy and keep him under our feet. We will be ignorant, to say the least, if we ignore what power God has given us, and worse than ignorant if we refuse to use those strategies to set others free from the bondage they experience because of the tongue. This book is a clear and effective way to deal with those things that cause you to struggle to overcome and enter into a life of abundance.

Pastor Deon Vanstaden
Gainesville, Georgia

Introduction

Ever wondered why you said something you shouldn't have said? Spoken "out of school?" Been carried away in an argument and wondered where those unkind and ungodly words that issued from your lips were coming from? Did it surprise you that a curse word sprang out of your mouth without forethought on your part? Have you ever wished you could "take back" something you said? Turn back the clock and start over in a conversation? If that's you, then this book is for you.

Would you like to change your circumstances and your life for the better? Improve your relationships and your health? Move effectively in the power of God? Become a spiritual powerhouse in God's kingdom? If that's you, then this book's for you.

As you read through these pages, you will discover that this is not simply another book about how to "tame the tongue" or how important our words are. It isn't simply an encouraging word, although you will be encouraged. This book is an in-depth look at how the enemy of our souls has deceived us into giving him the use of our tongues so that the very breath of God, which issues from our lungs, is used against God Himself.

The spirit realm is actually more real than the natural one in our lives because we are created as spirit beings with a mind, will, emotions and desires (a soul), living in human bodies. Other spirits, the Holy Spirit as well as spirits of darkness, want to express themselves through us. This book explains in plain terms how this happens.

Different evil spirits affect us in different ways (none of them good), and most of these spirits can be identified by the words they use. This book is a valuable weapon for spiritual warfare and provides a great reference tool as a sort of dictionary of the demonic.

The prayers at the end of each chapter are powerful! Read them out loud and engage your spirit in their truth. Why do I say to read them aloud? Only God can read our minds. His angels are on the alert to hearken to the "voice of the word of God" (Psalm 103:20, emphasis mine), and you and I are that voice. If the voice isn't heard, angels don't know to come and minister to us! Others that need to hear our godly prayers are Satan's demons. The host of hell is also on the alert to respond to our words, and we want them to hear and flee from God's word.

The three most important words in Christianity are, "It's my choice." It is so true that we have the choice as to whether or not we will receive life and blessings or death and curses. As we become free from the deceptions of the enemy, it becomes more clear to us how to choose the life and blessings we all want. Allow this book to bless you and free you today!

Vicki Smith Berdit

Realizing the Power in Our Words

"All the while my breath is in me, and the spirit of God is in my nostrils; My lips shall not speak wickedness, nor my tongue utter deceit."

Job 27:3-4

There have been thousands of messages about the power of words, and there have been lots of books written on the same subject. This one is designed to spark a power that can—and will—be applied into your life in a positive way. As you absorb this message, allow it to resonate in your spirit in such a way as to transform your life. We want to impart this truth so clearly that the understanding of it is unmistakable, and the bondage of the enemy can be finally and completely broken off your life.

Let this be our mutual goal: to thoroughly understand the power of our words, why they are powerful, how we fall victim to the wiles of the enemy, and how to separate ourselves from his influence by transforming our mouths into oracles of God.

Let's begin with a word from the Book of Job: *"Teach me, and I will hold my tongue: and cause me to understand wherein I have erred"* (Job 6:24).

Throughout this book, we're going to be led by the Holy Spirit to understand *"wherein we have erred."* We will be taught by the Holy Spirit to hold our tongues and examine our words in order to expose the wiles of the enemy in the area of spoken words. The Word of God tells us we should withstand the schemes of the enemy:

"Put on the whole armour of God, that you may be able to stand against the wiles of the devil" (Ephesians 6:11).

We are also told in the Word that we should not be ignorant of how Satan thinks or fail to understand his methods:

"Lest Satan should get an advantage of us: for we are not ignorant of his devices" (2 Corinthians 2:11).

Our words can be easily manipulated by the enemy to cause chaos and confusion, strife and contention, pain and heartache. Our own words can become a primary stronghold from which the devil can operate to capture and control us. Our own words can empower the enemy of our souls! You may ask, "How can that be true?" But you have only to look at your life to know that it is. The Word of God testifies over and over and over again about the power we hold in our tongues. Perhaps the most-quoted scripture regarding this is in Proverbs: *"Death and life are in the power of the tongue: and they that love it shall eat the fruit thereof"* (Proverbs 18:21).

We have all heard this, and most of us have used it on others more than once! Notice that it reads death and life, not life and death, are in the power of the tongue. Used by the enemy, our words can kill us and others. Jesus said it's not what goes into the mouth that defiles a man, but what comes out of it! Knowing that, we can also surmise that if we hold our tongue from speaking death, we can preserve our lives and enjoy prosperity in every area. That's what Job was saying in Job 6:24: *"Teach me, and I will hold my tongue."* Living the abundant life Jesus wants for us has a lot to do with what comes out of our mouths. Learning to speak life and not death involves recognizing the voice of the enemy and the many evil spirits behind the voice. As we progress in this study, we will specifically identify, by the words we speak, some of the evil spirits that are working in our hearts. Satan knows the power of the spoken word and seeks to use God's own power against Him. Unfortunately, we are far too eager to

help our enemy simply because we do not realize what
we are doing.

> My people are destroyed for lack of
> knowledge: because thou hast rejected
> knowledge, I will also reject thee, that thou
> shall be no priest to me: seeing thou hast
> forgotten the law of thy God, I will also
> forget thy children.
>
> Hosea 4:6

This scripture in Hosea applies to us in so many
ways, our words being a primary area. One of the
things these words tell us is that we can be the source
of a generational curse. One way that happens is
through what we release from our mouths into the
spiritual atmosphere. What we speak, our words,
can be a channel for the forces of hell! So what is it
that gives our words such spiritual impact? Why is
it that what we say can determine the outcome of a
circumstance for good or for evil, or set in motion a
situation for good or for evil?

The answer lies in Genesis: *"And the Lord God formed
man of the dust of the ground, and breathed into his nostrils
the breath of life; and man became a living soul"* (Genesis
2:7).

Every person on the planet is breathing with the breath of God. It is God's word, carried on His breath, that formed the world and everything in it. It is God's breath that carries our words. It is God's breath that gives life to the words we speak, the words that can build up or destroy, bless or curse, bring life or death. Our words are carried on the breath of God, and that makes them the most creative force in the universe! This is why Satan loves for us to speak words that oppose God's word in us, and so he assigns his henchmen demons to goad us into voicing his words rather than God's word.

> Even so the tongue is a little member, and
> boasts great things. Behold, how great a
> matter a little fire kindles! And the tongue
> is a fire, a world of iniquity: so is the tongue
> among our members, that it defiles the
> whole body, and sets on fire the course of
> nature; and it is set on fire of hell.
>
> James 3:5-6

These words in James clearly tell us our words defile us, and they can come from hell itself. The tongue is "set on fire of hell"! Demonic spirits are using our tongues to accomplish their destructive purposes. Here's the bottom line: mankind has dominion. The devil wants it. The easiest way to get it is to have us give it over to him through our words. Each of us must realize: "It's my choice."

All power belongs to God; Scripture is clear on that. Scripture is also clear that Jesus gave us the authority to use His power, and He gave us instruction as to what to do with it.

> And Jesus came and spake unto them, saying, All power is given unto me in heaven and in earth. Go ye therefore, and teach all nations, baptizing them in the name of the Father [immerse the people in the love of God] and of the Son [immerse the people in the soundness of Christ], and of the Holy Spirit [immerse the people in the power of God]: Teaching them to observe all things whatsoever I have commanded you: and, lo, I am with you always, even to the end of the world. Amen.
>
> Matthew 28:18-20
> hereinafter, text in brackets mine

What are those "whatsoever things" we are commanded to do? They are the actions that demonstrate the kingdom of God.

"And as ye go, preach, saying, The kingdom of heaven is at hand. Heal the sick, cleanse the lepers, raise the dead, cast out devils; freely ye have received, freely give" (Matthew 10:7-8).

So it becomes evident that we can use the power of God through the spoken word to destroy the works of the devil—sin, sickness, poverty, and death—just as Jesus did. Or we can give the power of the spoken word over to the enemy of our souls to use to destroy the works of God in our lives and the lives of others. It's our choice.

"For thy mouth uttereth thine iniquity, and thou choosest the tongue of the crafty" (Job 15:5).

Now that we're all getting a glimpse of the importance of our words, let's paint the picture with a little more detail. We want everyone to fully understand how God feels about what we say and to have enough information to agree with the spirit of God in this matter of what comes out of our mouths. God tells us in His Word that when we pray, we should speak the solution and not the problem:

> Be careful for nothing; but in everything by prayer and supplication with thanksgiving let your requests be made known to God."
>
> Philippians 4:6

In other words, thank the Lord in advance for your request, knowing it has already been provided for by the blood of Jesus.

Our prayers don't need to be gripe sessions with the Lord. As a matter of fact, God doesn't like complainers and murmurers. Remember Korah and Dathan and Abiram (Numbers 16)? They didn't like the way God put someone else in charge over them. They murmured and complained and finally spoke their complaint out before Moses. End result? The earth opened up and swallowed them, their families, and their possessions. The complaint department in heaven is closed, folks. We don't need to tell God what's wrong in our lives, He already knows. It isn't necessary to tell Him what we need. He already knows.

> But when ye pray, use not vain repetitions,
> as the heathen do: for they think that they
> shall be heard for their much speaking. Be
> not ye therefore like unto them: for your
> Father knoweth what things ye have need of,
> before ye ask him.
> Matthew 6:7-8

Let's move on. The Lord gives us examples in His Word of speaking prophetically and bringing the promises of God into existence, thus converting them from promises into benefits.

> Therefore it is of faith, that it might be by
> grace; to the end the promise might be sure
> to all the seed; not to that only which is of
> the law, [meaning of Moses, the natural
> Jew] but to that also which is of the faith of
> Abraham; who is the father of us all, (As it is
> written, I have made you a father of many
> nations,) before him whom he believed, even
> God, who quickens the dead, and calls those
> things which be not as though they were.
>
> Romans 4:16-17

In other words, be positively creative, not negatively creative, with our prophecies. Agree with God that He is faithful to His promises.

Think of this: even the birth, life, death, and resurrection of the Lord Jesus had to be spoken into existence by the prophets! There are dozens of scriptural references that speak this truth. How many times does the Bible say this thing or that thing happened that it "might be fulfilled" what was said by a prophet? In just a cursory look, I found fifty-nine, but there are probably more, depending on the different ways that phrase can be stated. We are to discover

God's plan, agree with God's plan, and speak God's plan into existence!

Speaking things into existence works both ways, however. Job got up every day, making a sacrifice to the Lord because he feared his children were partying too much or otherwise stepping out from under God's protection. Fear took the occasion of Job's negative and doubting supplication to God and actually brought his words to pass. One day, they were all eating and drinking together in the oldest brother's house, and boom, the house caved in from a windstorm and killed them all. We need to watch the condition of our hearts when we speak, even if it's to the Lord in prayer!

How many times have we said, "I'm getting sick," and then actually got sick? The Word even points out that we call affliction onto ourselves! Here's the progression of evil: a thought comes to us as the enemy speaks, either inwardly or through something we hear or see in the world, then we ponder the thought and begin to line up with it; we believe it. Next, we speak it out, and our declaration gives the enemy the right to make it happen.

"I believed, therefore have I spoken: I was greatly afflicted" (Psalm 116:10).

"Thou givest thy mouth to evil, and thy tongue frameth deceit" (Psalm 50:19).

Spiritual forces, both God's ministering angels and the devil's minions, are on the alert to work with our words and fulfill them. This is why both the Holy Spirit and the devil's demons want to possess our words! God wants us to speak His Word, which releases and empowers the angelic:

"Bless the LORD, ye his angels, that excel in strength, that do his commandments, hearkening unto the voice of his word" (Psalm 103:20).

Satan wants us to speak his word, which releases and empowers the demonic: *"He that hath a froward heart findeth no good: and he that hath a perverse tongue falleth into mischief"* (Proverbs 17:20).

We've all heard the expression "the weight of our words." Words have weight. They can burden and wear us down, causing confusion and shame: *"My confusion is continually before me, and the shame of my face hath covered me, For the voice of him that reproacheth and blasphemeth; by reason of the enemy and avenger"* (Psalm 44:15-16).

Conversely, our words can sustain and lift us up.

"A man shall eat good by the fruit of his mouth: but the soul of the transgressors shall eat violence" (Proverbs 13:2).

"A wholesome tongue is a tree of life: but perverseness therein is a breach in the spirit" (Proverbs 15:4).

We can state unquestionably that God has not been silent about the importance of our words. He has shown us the power of words and given us examples of how we are to speak. Since it's our choice as to what we allow to come out of our mouths and we have been told how to frame our speech, it's no wonder that God will hold us accountable for our words. There is a consequence to our words in the natural world, in this life we live right now, and there is a future consequence to our words.

> O generation of vipers, how can ye, being evil, speak good things? for out of the abundance of the heart the mouth speaketh. A good man out of the good treasure of the heart bringeth forth good things: and an evil man out of the evil treasure bringeth forth evil things. But I say unto you, That every idle word that men shall speak, they shall give account thereof in the day of judgment. For by thy words thou shalt be justified, and by thy words thou shalt be condemned.
>
> Matthew 12:34-37

This scripture is multidimensional, meaning it has truth for both today and tomorrow and truth in both the natural and the spiritual realms. The idle words we speak, useless things we say that are not of God, can bring condemnation into our lives in the natural realm, while speaking God's Word can enforce our righteousness in the spirit realm. Why is there a consequence now? Because today is the day of judgment. Yes, we know there will be a day when all who have confessed Jesus Christ as the Lord of their lives will stand before Him to receive rewards for how they've lived. But are we not to judge ourselves now? (We are not to judge each other, only ourselves.)

"For the time is come that judgment must begin at the house of God: and if it first begin at us, what shall the end be of them that obey not the gospel of God?" (1 Peter 4:17).

> Judge not, that ye be not judged. For with what judgment ye judge, ye shall be judged: and with what measure ye mete, it shall be measured to you again. And why beholdest thou the mote that is in thy brother's eye, but considerest not the beam that is in thine own eye? Or how wilt thou say to thy brother, Let me pull out the mote out of thine eye; and, behold, a beam is in thine own eye? Thou hypocrite, first cast out the beam out of thine own eye; and then shalt thou see clearly to cast out the mote out of thy brother's eye.
>
> Matthew 7:1-5

Each one of us is now the house of God, the dwelling place of His abiding presence. Judgment should begin in our own hearts as to where our words originate, not in pointing out the evil conversation of another. We need to have a critical view of what we say, even in jest, or maybe especially in jest, because once the words are released, they are eternal. And if our words carry anything at all that the devil can work with, he will!

"Thou art snared with the words of thy mouth, thou art taken with the words of thy mouth" (Proverbs 6:2).

We just made a comment about words spoken in jest. Personally, I don't believe we can say too much about the impact of words, especially the things we say following a potentially damaging comment or observation about someone, things like: "I was just kidding!" "Lighten up!" "Can't you take a joke?" Glossing over our words with follow-up comments such as these does not remove the words from the spiritual atmosphere.

I followed a study once on married couples who were continually digging at each other, all in fun, of course, and what we found was a higher than usual incidence of divorce, depression, and illness in couples who "kid around" with each other. Their spoken words, even when they were not intended to hurt, penetrated the spirits of the individuals and set up a pattern of destruction that brought division between them and tore down the relationship.

> Come, ye children, hearken unto me: I will teach you the fear of the LORD. What man is he that desireth life, and loveth many days, that he may see good? Keep thy tongue from evil, and thy lips from speaking guile.
>
> Psalm 34:11-13

We should all do our best not to speak ill of anyone, even as a joke. None of us may be completely free of the propensity toward coarse jesting, but even if it's a joke, it's a bad one, and the Lord doesn't like it.

> Be ye therefore followers of God, as dear children; And walk in love, as Christ also hath loved us, and hath given himself for us an offering and a sacrifice to God for a sweetsmelling savour. But fornication, and all uncleanness, or covetousness, let it not be once named among you, as becometh saints; Neither filthiness, nor foolish talking, nor jesting, which are not convenient: but rather giving of thanks.
>
> Ephesians 5:1-4

We also stopped playing April Fool's jokes, which fall into the category of jesting, when we found out the spiritual impact.

"As a mad man who casts firebrands, arrows, and death, So is the man that deceives his neighbour, and says, Am not I in sport?" (Proverbs 26:18-19).

Gossip is another idle use of our words that can bring destruction into people's lives. It fuels the fires of strife and division.

> Where no wood is, there the fire goes out: so where there is no talebearer, the strife ceases. As coals are to burning coals, and wood to fire; so is a contentious man to kindle strife. The words of a talebearer are as wounds, and they go down into the innermost parts of the belly.
>
> Proverbs 26:20-22

This is not to say we can't break the power of curses we speak or have spoken. When we allow the devil to trick us into speaking his word, we can cancel that word by pulling it down from the heavenlies, casting it to the ground, commanding it to die, and declaring it will bear no evil fruit. Our words can bring evil into our lives, and our words can destroy evil.

"He shutteth his eyes to devise froward things: moving his lips he bringeth evil to pass" (Proverbs 16:30).

Changing our patterns of bantering with our friends and family can make a tremendous difference in the relationships we have with them—a positive difference. For some of us, it may take a good bit of work. The devil has trained us to speak his words and criticize others if they don't "get it" that we didn't really mean anything by what we just said; it was simply meant to be funny.

We also put labels on ourselves and other people with our words, though most times not intentionally. We will say something like, "I'm stupid when it comes to..." or "I'm fat," or "ugly," or whatever derogatory thing comes to mind. Let's understand that those are words of the enemy and not God. Who's using your tongue?

It can be frustrating when a person is what we consider "out to lunch" a lot of the time, but what we need to understand is that the more often we say to a person, "you just don't get it" or "you don't listen" or "you don't pay attention," the more we entrap the person in what we speak. How can we help someone out of a trap when we continue to hold them in it? Can you pull your pants up while you're standing on the cuffs? That's what we often do to ourselves and others with the words we allow to come out of our mouths. If you've wondered why you can't seem to overcome some things, maybe this is the reason.

As we go on, we're going to explore the spirit world and identify some characteristic traits and language—words and phrases—commonly used by specific evil spirits. When we know what evil spirits typically say, it makes it easier for us to recognize precisely what we're dealing with. Once exposed, the devil doesn't stand a chance! Let's get started on the road to recovery from having our tongues hijacked. Let's declare the word of the living God over our speech!

Father God, thank You for showing so clearly that I can change my life by changing my words. Thank You, Lord, that You make a way where there seems to be no way and it's not hard to find or difficult to get to. Because of You, Lord, I can overcome my mouth. I can learn to take my words captive just as I do my thoughts, examine them, and reject those that don't line up with You, Your love, Your goodness, Your mercy, Your grace. Thank You that You are teaching me to recognize that evil spirits have infiltrated my speech, and thank You that You bring me deliverance from them. I thank You, Father, that You deliver my soul from lying lips and a deceitful tongue. I declare to You right now that with Your help, I will refrain my tongue from evil and my lips from speaking guile. I declare that while I live, my lips shall not speak wickedness, and my tongue will not utter deceit. Keep me, Lord, in Your will and Your way, in my speech, my actions, and my attitudes, in the name of Jesus. Amen.

Realizing the Power
in Hearing

"Who among you will give ear to this? who
will hearken and hear for the time to come?"
                                        Isaiah 42:23

"Incline your ear, and come unto me: hear,
and your soul shall live; and I will make an
everlasting covenant with you, even the sure
mercies of David."
                                        Isaiah 55:3

Looking at the power of hearing may seem at first
to be a strange topic in the subject of who's using
your tongue. However, speaking is only a part of what
we should know concerning languages, both in the
spirit world and in the natural world. Yes, what we
have already learned is absolutely true: our words are
creative and can cause both good and evil to come into

our lives. We empower good and can set in motion the plan of God by our words. We also empower evil and can set in motion the plan of the enemy by our words. Remember the scripture in James that tells us the tongue *"is set on fire of hell"!* But there is more to the power of words than speaking them; there is also the power of writing them and the power of hearing them. So far, we've focused on discovering and fully comprehending the power of our words. Now we're going to focus on the words we hear, how we hear them, and the power of hearing.

Keep in mind our goal: to thoroughly understand the power of words, why they are powerful, how we fall victim to the wiles of the enemy, and how to separate ourselves from his influence by transforming our mouths into oracles of God.

When the Lord told me to write about hearing, I have to say I was a little disappointed because I had my own ideas of how to put this book together. I was going to jump right in with what evil spirits say and how to determine what spirit is speaking by revealing the words they typically use. But my disappointment was completely turned around as the Holy Spirit imparted this word from the Lord. What you are about to discover has tremendous relevance and is foundational to our subject of the tongue and the language of the spirit world. Keep your minds open to receive God's blessing because the Lord has something to say about those who refuse to listen:

> This evil people, which refuse to hear my
> words, which walk in the imagination of
> their heart, and walk after other gods, to
> serve them, and to worship them, shall even
> be as this girdle, which is good for nothing.
> Jeremiah 13:10

Ouch! I repented for wanting things my way, and you can, too. We are laying the foundation for truly understanding the specific language patterns of different spirits, which we'll get to later. When we do, you'll find it effective information you can really apply into your life because you have these first foundational truths about words: speaking, hearing, and writing.

Here we go:

I think everyone can agree that before a word can come out of our mouths, the word must first be in our thoughts and in our hearts. In order for that to happen, we have to hear. We hear things spiritually, and we hear things physically. We have two sets of ears: one for words we physically hear in the natural world and another for words we receive in our hearts through spirit-to-spirit communication. God wants us to receive His word by hearing Him in our spirit and then to "hear it," which means we must physically speak God's word for our physical ears to pick it up in the natural world. This is one reason it's valuable to read the Word of God out loud because when we do, we're getting it with both sets of ears!

"Moreover he said unto me, Son of man, all my words that I shall speak unto thee receive in thine heart, and hear with thine ears" (Ezekiel 3:10).

No matter what kind of word it is, we have to have received the word and tucked it away someplace in our hearts in order to speak it out. Words come from information we've received. So the question is: how did we get the information we are speaking?

The Bible tells us that information comes from three sources. Information comes from man, which speaks of our five senses (what we see and hear and touch and taste and feel), our experiences in the world, and what other people say. Information comes from the spirit of God, which speaks of the Holy Spirit gently teaching, guiding, and correcting us from within our hearts. And information comes from the devil, which speaks of Satan and his demons feeding us a point of view that opposes God and His plan and purpose for us. We see the biblical evidence of this most clearly in the discourse between Jesus and His disciples at the time when Jesus asked them, "Who am I?"

When Jesus came into the coasts of Caesarea
Philippi, he asked his disciples, saying,
Whom do men say that I the Son of man
am? And they said, Some say that thou art
John the Baptist: some, Elias; and others,
Jeremias, or one of the prophets.

> Matthew 16:13-14

Here is our first example of the different sources
of information that we can use to convert into words.
This is the experience of man: what we see in the
world, the comparisons we make, and what people say.
We hear what other people are saying and thinking;
we examine it for its reality, or maybe we take it as
real whether it is or not. We compare what we hear to
what has happened in our lives before and the cause
and effect we've experienced. If it all seems to make
sense in our warped thinking, we can then choose to
align with the general belief in the world and speak the
same words as other people are speaking. This is the
kind of reasoning that is considered to be "walking by
sight."

It's amazing how many times we take the word of
another person as truth, even from perfect strangers.
Have you ever struck up a conversation with someone
at the movie theater? Some of you have asked a person
you never met what they watched and whether or not

it was any good. What they answered played a part, not only in whether you decided to see that particular movie, but how much you yourself liked it when you did! We get information from the world, our experiences, and the experiences of others. We hear the word of the world, and too often, we act on the word of the world rather than waiting for the word of the Lord. Reading on:

> He saith unto them, But whom say ye that I am? And Simon Peter answered and said, Thou art the Christ, the Son of the living God. And Jesus answered and said unto him, Blessed art thou, Simon Barjona: for flesh and blood hath not revealed it unto thee, but my Father which is in heaven. And I say also unto thee, That thou art Peter, and upon this rock I will build my church; and the gates of hell shall not prevail against it. And I will give unto thee the keys of the kingdom of heaven: and whatsoever thou shalt bind on earth shall be bound in heaven: and whatsoever thou shalt loose on earth shall be loosed in heaven.
>
> Matthew 16:15-19

Here is the second source of information from which we frame our words. This is revelation knowledge from the throne room of heaven, the voice of the living God. It doesn't take a super spiritual person to know that this is the voice we want to hear! An interesting observation in this progression of hearing is that our first response, demonstrated by the disciples, is to hear the word of the world. We want to give an immediate response to what we are asked, based on what we see or hear or our past experiences. But Peter apparently didn't respond quickly to Jesus' question. He pondered the question and waited and was rewarded with revelation.

Peter got the word of God, not the word of the world. And Jesus pointed out the blessing in his, and our, doing that. There is great blessing in not speaking quickly, in not reacting to something from a position of what we know or think we know, but rather waiting and responding from a position of what God knows and reveals to us. Look at it! Jesus said, *"upon this rock"* (the rock of revelation knowledge, the Word of God), He would build His church, and the gates of hell cannot prevail against it. In other words, whatever words the enemy is pouring forth from hell cannot stand against the revelation knowledge of the Word of God.

Then charged he his disciples that they should tell no man that he was Jesus the Christ. From that time forth began Jesus to shew unto his disciples, how that he must go unto Jerusalem, and suffer many things of the elders and chief priests and scribes, and be killed, and be raised again the third day. Then Peter took him, and began to rebuke him, saying, Be it far from thee, Lord: this shall not be unto thee. But he turned, and said unto Peter, Get thee behind me, Satan: thou art an offence unto me: for thou savourest not the things that be of God, but those that be of men.

Matthew 16:20-23

Here is the third source of information we can choose to hear, the voice of the enemy. Notice that Jesus didn't say, "Peter, you're thinking wrong." He said, *"Get thee behind me, Satan!"* He was telling Peter and us, "That's not even your thought; it did not originate with you." The devil will always speak in opposition to God's plan and purpose, whether it's the plan He has for restoration in our individual lives or within the greater plan of total restoration of the earth. If we are to fully avoid the devil's words, we must be fully aligned with the plan of God. There is only one thing that gets in the way of our being fully aligned with the plan of God, and that is "self." Think of Peter. He had the revelation knowledge from the Holy Spirit that Jesus is the Christ, the Son of the living God. After Peter received this revelation, Jesus told him and the other disciples God's plan. Why then, knowing by the spirit of God that Jesus is the Christ, would Peter deny that Jesus knew the plan of God and was following it? Why would he hear the word of the devil and choose to believe it and speak it?

The answer lies in our self-focus and pride. Those are two areas in which the devil has a perfect right to bring deception into our lives and out of our mouths. We know best, don't we! Who knows better than me what's best for me, and for you, too? Peter judged Jesus' explanation of what was about to happen as being not of God, even knowing Jesus was God! In his selfishness and pride, Peter heard the word of the devil, and it sounded good. It was selfishness because Peter didn't want to be without Jesus. He loved Jesus and didn't want Him to be killed. It was pride because Peter knew, as did all good Jewish people of the day, that the Messiah was supposed to liberate them from the oppression of the world, and he was expecting a worldly, not a spiritual, liberation. Obviously, in Peter's estimation, Jesus didn't get the right message, so he was bringing correction to the Lord.

We do that all the time. "Lord, I don't think You're doing this right. What's happening here isn't fair." We are so quick to think we have the answers! And because we want things our way, we tell God how things should be done, when things should be done, and to whom things should be done. We've often said that all Christians want to serve God, but most of us want to serve Him in an advisory manner. "Give me the job of chief counsel, Lord, and do things my way and in my time. That would be the right thing for You to do." If you can't say, "Amen," say, "Ouch."

In any case, we see three areas of information and can understand it's our choice as to what we hear, what we believe, whether we react hastily or respond thoughtfully, and how we assimilate and disseminate the information. How does what we hear affect us personally, and how does what we hear affect others through us? One meaning of the word "assimilate" is to take something in and make it a part of the thing it has joined. Whatever word we choose to hear, the word of the world, the word of the devil, or the word of God, we can assimilate that word into our being, and it becomes a part of who we are. We will then disseminate, which means "to spread abroad as though sowing seed,"[1] the word we've heard. The sower sows the seed; the seed is the word. What seeds are we sowing into our lives, our families, our communities, and even the world? We will sow what we have heard.

The little song we learned in Sunday school as children, "Be careful, little ears, what you hear," is as applicable to us as adults as it is to children, although we tend to think children may be more impressionable. I don't think they are; I just think they have less spiritual defense and are more likely to trust that everything they hear is true than we, grown-ups, do. That's a matter of experience, not gullibility. As we grow in the Lord, we should grow in spiritual discernment. What we hear can help us or hurt us in our growth because faith comes by hearing. What we hear is what we tend to believe. When we go to the doctor, are we more likely to hear his bad diagnosis and react to it, or are we more likely to go to Doctor Jesus, get His word on the matter, and respond to that instead?

When we come before God, we need to be more eager to listen than to speak. Instead of going to God and saying, "Oh, God, I've got cancer! How could You let this happen to me?" and pouring out a litany of problems and things that are wrong in our lives, and begging God to "do something about it," we need to go to God and say, "Father God, the doctor gave me this word, but what's Your word about it?" And then listen to hear what the Lord has to say.

Keep thy foot when thou goest to the house of God, and be more ready to hear, than to give the sacrifice of fools: for they consider not that they do evil. Be not rash with thy mouth, and let not thine heart be hasty to utter any thing before God: for God is in heaven, and thou upon earth: therefore let thy words be few.

Ecclesiastes 5:1-2

When we're busy talking, it's hard to hear what's being said by others, especially God. The devil doesn't want us to hear God and will put all sorts of distractions and hindrances in our heads and in our surroundings to prevent us from hearing. One of those hindrances is that we talk too much. We go into our prayer closets and begin to pour out our supplications, and that's not all bad, but understand that God says, "Hear Me." We can't hear when we're talking. There is a time to simply be quiet and listen rather than talk, talk, talk or pray, pray, pray. This goes back to one of the verses we've looked at before, from the book of Matthew: *"But when ye pray, use not vain repetitions, as the heathen do: for they think that they shall be heard for their much speaking"* (Matthew 6:7).

It is neither how much we say nor how long our prayers are that is important, it's our words and our hearts, and it's also our willingness to listen, to hearken, and obey what we hear when we are in the presence of God. The Lord says we should be ready and willing to hear His voice when He speaks to us. When the Lord gives us a positive, encouraging answer to a very negatively appearing situation about our health, family relationships, a business deal, or whatever, we need to receive that word, line up with His plan, and begin to speak it into existence. If we don't agree with the truth, we get to live in the lie! Just as Jesus told Peter that there is great blessing in getting revelation from the Holy Spirit, there is also a consequence if we refuse to hear, receive, and act on what the Holy Spirit reveals.

> I also will choose their delusions, and will bring their fears upon them; because when I called, none did answer; when I spake, they did not hear: but they did evil before mine eyes, and chose that in which I delighted not.
>
> Isaiah 66:4

None of us is eager to be under delusion, but this is not the only place in Scripture that the Lord says He will let us have delusion and do nothing to keep it from us. In this verse, God says He Himself will put His finger on the thing we believe that is in truth a delusion and bring it to pass because we have chosen to hear the lie and not the truth. God will leave us to our own devices if that is what we choose.

> Even him, whose coming is after the working of Satan with all power and signs and lying wonders, And with all deceivableness of unrighteousness in them that perish; because they received not the love of the truth, that they might be saved. And for this cause God shall send them strong delusion, that they should believe a lie: That they all might be damned who believed not the truth, but had pleasure in unrighteousness.
>
> 2 Thessalonians 2:9-12

When we choose to believe what we hear in the world rather than what God says, we can have the things of the world, which are cursed, rather than the things of God, which are blessed. It has to do with hearing and receiving the truth in our hearts. We should ask the Lord to give us ears to hear His truth and hearts that receive, understand, and love the truth. Having ears to hear is a characteristic of the overcomer. Having ears to hear will also provide sustenance and abundant life in the presence of God, both now and for all eternity.

"He that hath an ear, let him hear what the Spirit saith unto the churches; To him that overcometh will I give to eat of the tree of life, which is in the midst of the paradise of God" (Revelation 2:7).

We need to be listening to what the Holy Spirit has to say and close our ears to the spirit of the world and the voice of the enemy. Then we will have more understanding of God's plan and can advance His plan more easily on the earth and in our individual lives. We will also gain a greater understanding of vision and begin to see things God's way and not our own way. We tend to think there are three ways of viewing things: God's way, my way, and the devil's way. But while there may be a speck of truth in that thought, it's not the truth. There are only two ways: God's way is one. Everything else is the devil's way because anytime we don't agree with God, Satan will take that as an agreement with him. The result is the same. We're off track and headed for destruction.

"There is a way that seemeth right unto a man, but the end thereof are the ways of death" (Proverbs 16:25).

"When my spirit was overwhelmed within me, then thou knewest my path. In the way wherein I walked have they privily laid a snare for me" (Psalm 142:3).

Going our own way in the spirit of the world, hearing the words of the world, and speaking the words of the world makes us vulnerable to the schemes and entrapments of the enemy. If I'm going my own way, I can expect the enemy to lay a trap for me. God says it. I believe it. And wisdom tells me to go His way, and not mine. I am to hear His truth, respond to His truth, speak His truth, and stay out of trouble.

There's another area of words to look at briefly, and that is the written word. A simple progression to bringing something to pass is this: decide, declare, decree. We decide the thing in our heart, we declare it by speaking prophetically with our tongue, and we decree it by writing it down. The written and sealed decree of a king cannot be reversed. A higher decree can be written, but nothing can change the one before it. A covenant can't be undone, although a higher covenant can supersede the one before it. One of the biblical examples of a written decree and its significance as irreversible is in the book of Esther. As you recall, wicked Haman had written a decree that all the Jewish people were to be killed on a certain day and sealed the decree with the king's signet. Esther came before King Ahasuerus to seek a reversal of the king's decree after Haman's wickedness was discovered and Haman had been hanged. Notice that even though the decree was done by Haman, under trickery which made it fraudulent, it stood. Once the decree had gone out, nothing could stop it.

Then the king held out the golden sceptre toward Esther. So Esther arose, and stood before the king, And said, If it please the king, and if I have found favour in his sight, and the thing seem right before the king, and I be pleasing in his eyes, let it be written to reverse the letters devised by Haman the son of Hammedatha the Agagite, which he wrote to destroy the Jews which are in all the king's provinces: For how can I endure to see the evil that shall come unto my people? or how can I endure to see the destruction of my kindred? Then the king Ahasuerus said unto Esther the queen and to Mordecai the Jew, Behold, I have given Esther the house of Haman, and him they have hanged upon the gallows, because he laid his hand upon the Jews. Write ye also for the Jews, as it liketh you, in the king's name, and seal it with the king's ring: for the writing which is written in the king's name, and sealed with the king's ring, may no man reverse.

Esther 8:4-8

Here we see that not even the king himself could reverse his own written decree. But he could write another, higher decree. In this particular case, the decree was that the Jews could defend themselves against anyone who came against them for harm. That settled the issue because no one was willing to kill someone who might kill them instead! End of the problem.

Another great example of the significance of the written word is in Habakkuk.

> I will stand upon my watch, and set me upon the tower, and will watch to see what he will say unto me, and what I shall answer when I am reproved. And the LORD answered me, and said, Write the vision, and make it plain upon tables, that he may run that readeth it.
>
> Habakkuk 2:1-2

Here we see the prophet waiting on the Lord, listening for the Lord, hearing the word of the Lord, and being instructed to write it down. There are a few things to note from this passage about hearing the Lord. "Standing on our watch" means being in our appointed place, steadfast in our assignment. "Setting ourselves on the tower and watching" means positioning ourselves and leaning toward the Lord, inclining our ears to His word, and being ready to receive it.

So here we are, in our place, fulfilling our assignment and stepping into a place to receive and obey God's word. It is then that He gives us His vision and says, "Write it down." Make a written decree and make it clear so that you and others, whoever reads it, can also agree and set about making it happen. Write the vision. Decree the decree that God has given you!

The written word, just as the spoken word, has weight. Don't think that demons can't read. The written word that opposes God can set evil in motion and bring evil into existence, just as the spoken word can. For good or for evil, the words we hear and then write down will impact our lives. This is why it may not be a good idea to do "journaling." When we write down bad feelings, "I was so depressed today," or curses people spoke over us, "My boyfriend said I'm fat," our words can become a decree that cannot be reversed. They may hold certain unpleasant things in place until we overcome them by a higher decree and words that agree with God's opinion and not the world or other people.

Is it always bad to keep a journal? Maybe not, but our suggestion is a prayer journal or a dream journal with godly interpretations or the word of the Lord that comes to you in prophecy or prayer. Then you can review it periodically and be reminded of how God has moved in your life. But recording the everyday "he said, she said" is probably not a good thing. That is documentation that does not need to be kept unless you may be asked for it in a court of law or for some similar purpose. Businesses need to keep documentation; medical professions need to keep documentation, and so forth. But also know that a written medical diagnosis is both good and bad. It gives us specifics that we can pray against, but it is also a written decree. We have canceled medical records in the spirit realm and seen improvement in people's health.

The conclusion of all this is: be cautious in what you hear and in what you write. Listen to the Lord and His report. Accept it, believe it, respond to it, and watch it change your life in a positive way. God only wants the best for us, and many things that have happened in our lives were not in His plan for us. The words we heard as children, words that made us feel worthless and unwanted, were not God's words. Because we accepted them, believed them, and reacted to them, we've opened doors of demonic subjection. Now we must learn to close those doors, and the quickest way to do that is by hearing, speaking, and writing God's opinion. Stand on your watch, set yourself in a place to hear from God, then hearken and obey the word you receive.

"Now ye are clean through the word which I have spoken unto you" (John 15:3).

For us to be clean by the word the Lord speaks, we must be willing to hear it.

Father, I thank You that You have given me ears to hear Your voice, and I ask Your help in standing my watch so that I can position myself to hear You clearly and respond appropriately. Help me daily recognize what voice I'm hearing, and when I hear the spirit of the world or the words of the devil, help me tune them out and turn back to You. Help me recognize Your truth, Lord, so that I am not in delusion. Help me discern the lie of the enemy and not agree with it. Keep me from being hasty with my words, help me thoughtfully examine everything I hear, and sow only good seeds with my words, seeds that will bring forth fruits worthy of repentance and show my love for You and my heart of gratitude toward You. Remove far from me the spirit of selfishness that would cause me to reject Your plans and purposes and remove the pride that causes me to think I know better than You do how things should be. Make my words few, Lord, but powerful, to accomplish Your plans, not mine. Keep me and my words in Your way and remove my foot and my lips from an unclean way that seems right but leads to destruction and despair. I declare to You, Father God: I want only Your words emanating from my lips, bringing blessings into my life, my family, and the world; I purpose in my heart to be aware of what I hear and to discard those words that oppose You. Give me fresh vision, Lord, from Your point of view. I want to see things the way You see them. I will write the vision, make it plain, and I will run with it to see Your plan accomplished, Your church in unity, and the earth restored by Your word in my ears, in my heart, and on my lips. In the name of Jesus. Amen.

Exploring the Language of the Spiritual Realm

"The transgression of the wicked saith
within my heart, that there is no fear of God
before his eyes."

Psalm 36:1

We are now going to begin discovering the
language of the spirit world in order to determine
which evil spirits we may be encountering based on
the words we speak or the words we hear or read. So
far, we've explained how and why words are creative
and that words can cause both good and evil to come
into our lives. When we hear and speak God's words,
we empower good and set in motion the plan of God.
On the other hand, when we speak the words of the
enemy, we empower evil and set in motion the plan of

Satan. That makes it important to know what words the enemy uses.

There is a pattern to speech, whether it is cultural, geographical, social, or spiritual. This is why it's important to know a bit about the culture when visiting a foreign country. If you use words and phrases unfamiliar to people because of cultural differences, they will have no idea what you're talking about. When we were in India, I was making a point about what we choose to listen to, and I said, "My ears are not garbage cans." The point was completely lost because they don't use garbage cans in the region we visited in India, which is a distinct cultural difference. The people just throw all their trash into piles outside, and then they burn the piles. In America, we'd know what was meant by the phrase "ears are not garbage cans": we don't listen to worthless things. In India, the response to that statement was a blank look of confusion on practically every face.

Geographical words and phrases are specific to an area. People from other parts of the country identify a southerner not just by the accent but by the words they use: "ya'll" is a giveaway that a person is from the south. "Ya'll come back now, you hear?"—that's usually indicative of a country-bred southerner.

Social words and phrases are specific to certain people groups. You don't normally relate "They have a great cocktail hour" to a conversation between poor people or see those words on the agenda for a church retreat.

Every industry has its own language, too. There are certain words and phrases that identify different professions or fields of business. Walk into a conversation between doctors on the job, and you could be completely lost in the medical jargon. The same is true with legalese between attorneys. If you hear or read "chiffonade" or "julienne," you know you're dealing with people who understand cooking descriptions. Unless you're a cowboy, you might not know that "This ain't my first rodeo" means "You can't fool me!" or that a "boil over" is when a horse starts bucking.

Language is specific, and just as specific words and phrases help us identify and locate different people groups, there are specific words and phrases that identify demons in the spiritual realm. In a general sense, we can say the words and phrases used by the demonic will always oppose the word of God. So when we hear something, either with our outer ears or as a thought in our inner ears, and it doesn't sound like something God says, we can know the enemy is at work to deceive us or lead us into fear. Demonic words are always designed to create chaos, confusion, contention, or some other unsettling feeling or situation, and they have an assignment of destruction; the enemy's goal is to kill, steal, and destroy. Words can be weapons of destruction used by demons to hinder the purposes of God.

It's not really difficult to recognize a word from the enemy when we know the Word of God. Words from the enemy are vain imaginations and high things meant to overthrow the truth. We are to cast down these vain imaginations and high things. We are not to react to them; we are to respond to God.

> For though we walk in the flesh, we do
> not war after the flesh: (For the weapons
> of our warfare are not carnal, but mighty
> through God to the pulling down of strong
> holds;) Casting down imaginations, and
> every high thing that exalteth itself against
> the knowledge of God, and bringing into
> captivity every thought to the obedience of
> Christ.
>
> 2 Corinthians 10:3-5

Most of us know the words that oppose God; at least we know them if we take a moment to examine them and compare them to the never-ending, everlasting, unfailing love words God speaks to us. But while we can recognize and say, "That's from the enemy," in order to separate ourselves from the effects of the words or a continuing barrage of heartache and hindrance, we need to know the enemy behind the words. Which of Satan's demonic henchmen is attempting to fulfill this particular assignment? Our goal is to expose the characteristic words and phrases of different evil spirits so that we are more able to separate ourselves from them and send them back to the pit of hell where they belong! Let's begin with a subject we all know, and that is *rejection*.

Identifying and Overcoming Rejection

**"He is despised and rejected of men; a man
of sorrows, and acquainted with grief: and
we hid as it were our faces from him; he was
despised, and we esteemed him not."**

Isaiah 53:3

Rejection is a form of communication, and we
can all experience it daily, on one side or the other.
You and I, and every other person on the planet, have
the opportunity to be rejected, or to reject someone
else, every single day. Some of us live in rejection to
the degree that it becomes a way of life. It's become a
comfort zone, and we feel strangely safe in it. We say
we don't like it but actually do very little to change the
situation. Instead, we continue to participate with

rejection and continue to allow it to control our lives. For example, we can't develop relationships because we've been rejected so many times we've allowed that nasty spirit to teach us to reject the ones we love as a defense mechanism against the hurt of being rejected by them. It's just crazy the way we let the devil have his way, and all the while, we think it's what we really want! That's true deception.

When rejection speaks, it can be through words, actions, even a look; and even though we're looking specifically at words, we should realize that looks and actions often have words behind them, those thoughts in our minds. Most of us spend way too much time thinking about what someone else might be thinking about us. We're going to share with you a little story about a married couple and how sneaky rejection is and how it starts a progression of unloving thoughts that lead to destruction. We'll call this couple John and Marsha. Marsha has a history of rejection...she never felt loved by her father or accepted by her family. She's been divorced more than once because the men she chose rejected her so that they could be with someone else. Now she has a wonderful husband! Maybe he's a little oblivious to her feelings at times, but he loves her and is a faithful husband. Here's the scenario:

John gets up in the morning after a night of staying up late watching football, and Marsha notices that he seems preoccupied. "What's wrong, honey?" she asks. "Nothing," he mumbles and continues getting ready for work. Marsha tries more than once to engage John in conversation, but he gives her short answers and then hides behind the sports page at the breakfast table. The enemy begins to work on Marsha, bringing doubts into her mind: "I wonder what's wrong with John. He's so distant. Maybe I did something wrong. I wonder what I did. I bet he's mad because I went shopping with Mary yesterday, so he's giving me the silent treatment."

As the day progresses, Marsha decides to "make it up" to John. She's already decided he's mad at her. She's already thought of the reason behind his silence. So she cooks John's favorite meal, lights the candles, and gets herself ready for a romantic evening with her husband. John comes home from work and sits down to dinner. He doesn't seem to notice the perfume or the candles or that he's eating his favorite meal.

Marsha continues to try to get John to talk to her. He's pretty much unresponsive, and so she cuddles next to him after dinner and makes sensual advances. They go to bed and have a wonderful encounter, but when Marsha says, "I love you, John," he responds with some sort of male-type grunt. Marsha begins to cry softly. John doesn't notice.

Rejection begins to speak: "John didn't say he loves me. John doesn't love me anymore. He didn't care that I made his favorite meal, and he didn't notice the candles and perfume. This is more than just my shopping spree. He's got another woman. That's the only reason he'd act this way! Well, that does it. Tomorrow I see an attorney. I'll show him he can't dump me like this; let's see if she will make him his favorite meal! He'll be sorry when I'm gone."

On the other side of the bed, John is drifting into a sweet sleep. He's thinking, *Well, the Patriots lost yesterday, but at least Marsha didn't have a headache.*

This may seem to be a ridiculous exaggeration, but it's a great example. In this case, the spirit of rejection that Marsha had carried around since childhood took yet another occasion to talk to her. Notice that this evil spirit spoke in the first person so Marsha would accept its evil promptings as her own thoughts. Rejection helped her come to a false conclusion that would cause her to reject her husband and her own happiness. It happens every day. It's interesting to note that John *did not* reject his wife. He didn't say anything to reject her or her advances, and yet Marsha felt rejection because of his unresponsiveness toward her. She wasn't invited into his thoughts about football and the disappointment he felt because his team lost, so she felt discarded.

We could probably say with some degree of accuracy that John didn't share his thoughts about the football game with Marsha because of his own fear of rejection. If he had admitted and exposed his feelings of disappointment, she might have rejected his feelings as not valid or just plain silly. ("My goodness, it's only a game!") It happens.

In this example, the words of rejection were played out in Marsha's thoughts. Her past experience of having a husband leave her for another woman gave the spirit of rejection a plausible foundation for demonic words of rejection to rule over the truth that John is a faithful husband who loves her. Marsha had been trained by rejection and easily participated in its suggestions, falling in line with a word opposing God's Word.

To recognize rejection, we must be aware of its goal. The goal of rejection is to reject. It wants us to reject ourselves, reject others, and reject God. It wants us to reject opportunities and blessings and live in misery and isolation, unable to advance the kingdom of God because we've believed the lies that rejection tells us. Rejection works, and sometimes speaks, in concert with other unloving spirits to disagree with everything God says about us. It exalts man's opinion over God's opinion, and that opens the door to idolatry. When we receive and accept words of rejection that other people say about us, we are, in fact, believing and worshipping another god, that god being a flesh and blood man or woman who just put us down.

When we agree with rejection, we are saying that we know more about ourselves than God knows about us. Agreeing with words of rejection that oppose God's word is the same as saying that God is a liar. Receiving and accepting words of rejection as truth is a practice that becomes a habit that denies the cross.

We started out with a verse in Isaiah about Jesus Christ, "He was despised and rejected of men." And not only men but God! When God turned His face from Him because of the sin He bore on our behalf, Jesus took rejection that you and I will never experience. Why was Jesus rejected? So that we could be accepted. There is a divine exchange available because of the cross of the Lord Jesus Christ. Every time someone rejects us, we can choose to make the exchange by giving the rejection to Jesus and receiving His total acceptance. It's our choice.

Most of us know the words of rejection very well, but I think it's good to go over a few of them and craft an answer to close the mouth of the liar named rejection. When Jesus was tempted by Satan, He answered the temptations with the Word of God, "It is written..." We need to do the same things Jesus did when confronted with the temptation of accepting rejection, answer with the Word of God.

The first words of rejection to attack our identity and cause feelings of shame that hinder us are in the category of character assassination. These are words and phrases such as "worthless," "good for nothing," "lowlife," "loser," and "never going to make it." What is God's answer to these demonic words of rejection?

Rejection says: "I am worthless."

God says: *"For thou art an holy people unto the LORD thy God, and the LORD hath chosen thee to be a peculiar people unto himself, above all the nations that are upon the earth"* (Deuteronomy 14:2).

> Are not two sparrows sold for a farthing? and one of them shall not fall on the ground without your Father. But the very hairs of your head are all numbered. Fear ye not therefore, ye are of more value than many sparrows.
>
> Matthew 10:29-31

In the verse in Deuteronomy, and in other places, God's word to us is that we are a treasure, a wealth preserved unto Him for His purpose. In Matthew, Jesus Himself confirms that we have value. We are so precious to the Lord that He knows the number of hairs on our heads, saying that everything about us, even those things we don't think about, everything about us has value and is important to God.

Rejection says: "I am good for nothing."

God says: *"Before I formed thee in the belly I knew thee; and before thou camest forth out of the womb I sanctified thee, and I ordained thee a prophet unto the nations"* (Jeremiah 1:5).

> Who hath saved us, and called us with an
> holy calling, not according to our works, but
> according to his own purpose and grace,
> which was given us in Christ Jesus before the
> world began.
>
> 2 Timothy 1:9

According to the Word of God, He has a plan and purpose for each one of us. We are called with a holy calling, and we are appointed from before birth to our calling in God. We should all remember that not even man creates something without a purpose. God did not create us and then say, "Oh, my! What am I going to do with this one?" Every one of us was created by God with purpose and a calling. He gives us what we need to fulfill our calling. God does not change His mind about it or take back the talents and abilities

He's put within us. *"For the gifts and calling of God are without repentance"* (Romans 11:29).

Rejection says: "I am a low-life creature."

God says:

> And the LORD hath avouched thee this
> day to be his peculiar people, as he hath
> promised thee, and that thou shouldest keep
> all his commandments; And to make thee
> high above all nations which he hath made,
> in praise, and in name, and in honour; and
> that thou mayest be an holy people unto the
> LORD thy God, as he hath spoken.
>
> Deuteronomy 26:18-19

> It is God that avengeth me, and that bringeth
> down the people under me, And that
> bringeth me forth from mine enemies: thou
> also hast lifted me up on high above them
> that rose up against me: thou hast delivered
> me from the violent man.
>
> 2 Samuel 22:48-49

Again we can see ourselves in God's Word as a special treasure that He defends and lifts high above others. There is nothing base about us or our lives. The poor and humble are exalted by God. We don't have to buckle under to the rejections of the world because we don't have what other people might have. God is our portion and the strength of our hearts when we are reviled.

"But thou, O LORD, art a shield for me; my glory, and the lifter up of mine head" (Psalm 3:3).

"My flesh and my heart faileth: but God is the strength of my heart, and my portion for ever" (Psalm 73:26).

Rejection says: "I'm a loser."

God says:

> Who shall separate us from the love of Christ? shall tribulation, or distress, or persecution, or famine, or nakedness, or peril, or sword? As it is written, For thy sake we are killed all the day long; we are accounted as sheep for the slaughter. Nay, in all these things we are more than conquerors through him that loved us.
>
> Romans 8:35-37

God says we are more than conquerors, that we have victory over trouble, anxiety, stress, persecution, famine, poverty, danger, and even death...all because of the cross. The blood of the Lord Jesus Christ has freed us from being losers and elevated us to a place of authority over the beggarly elements of life.

Why would we choose to agree with rejection and go back into victimization to accept the label of "loser?"

> Howbeit then, when ye knew not God, ye did service unto them which by nature are no gods. But now, after that ye have known God, or rather are known of God, how turn ye again to the weak and beggarly elements, whereunto ye desire again to be in bondage?
> Galatians 4:8-9

Rejection says: "I'm never going to make it." (It will cause us to reject a project or idea simply because it convinces us we can't finish it.)

God says: *"Being confident of this very thing, that he which hath begun a good work in you will perform it until the day of Jesus Christ"* (Philippians 1:6).

Family members are those most likely to be used by a spirit of rejection to squelch our ambitions. They tell us all the reasons why we can't do something, and they point out all the other people who have tried the same thing and failed or the times we ourselves tried and failed at something. In business, bosses who have rejection issues in their lives may find they hire employees who do the same thing: they shoot down ideas, they make excuses as to why a project or a deadline is impossible. We need to realize that the plan of God will not fail. You and I are an integral part of the plan of God, which means as long as we are with Him, He will be with us. And when we stray away and return again, He is waiting to pick up where we left off and carry us on into His purpose. God started the work in us, and He will complete it. We will make it!

There are other categories of rejection. For instance, just as rejection uses character assassination to reject, rejection also assassinates physical appearance. Rejection says things like "ugly," "too fat," "four eyes," "bean pole," "string bean," "roly-poly," "dog," and "pig," and it disparages noses, ears, breasts, and other body parts. We probably don't need to name every insult we've ever heard or every name we've been called because we can all recognize words that attack physical appearance.

Rejection says: "I am unattractive. I am ugly."
God says:

> Thine eyes did see my substance, yet being unperfect; and in thy book all my members were written, which in continuance were fashioned, when as yet there was none of

them. How precious also are thy thoughts unto me, O God! how great is the sum of them!

Psalm 139:16-17

"Thou art beautiful, O my love, as Tirzah, comely as Jerusalem, terrible as an army with banners" (Song of Solomon 6:4).

God sees us as beautiful. If he thought we were "ugly," He wouldn't waste all those thoughts on us, now would He? We have only to read the Song of Solomon to know God is excited about us and that He wants intimacy with us. We have His admiration as well as His love. It really doesn't matter what people think about our looks or what we think the mirror says; God says we're beautiful and desirable.

Another category of rejection involves our abilities. Words that attack our abilities and are designed to render us ineffective and miserable include "dumber than a rock," "stupid," "moron," "imbecile," "incapable," "slow learner," "handicapped," "inadequate," "unable," "not good enough," "not smart enough," "too slow," "too clumsy," "two left feet," "can't walk and chew gum," "can't carry a tune in a bucket," "tone-deaf," and "can't do it." The number of people we've known who allowed rejection to put these labels on them is more than we can count offhand. When people believe the lie of rejection and accept its label, it creates an identity crisis that causes them to deny their own talents and abilities, and it sets them up for failure and more rejection.

Rejection says: "I'm dumb, stupid, an imbecile, and a moron."

God says: *"For who hath known the mind of the Lord, that he may instruct him? But we have the mind of Christ"* (1 Corinthians 2:16).

"But ye have an unction from the Holy One, and ye know all things" (1 John 2:20).

> Have not I written to thee excellent things
> in counsels and knowledge, That I might
> make thee know the certainty of the words of
> truth; that thou mightest answer the words
> of truth to them that send unto thee?
>
> Proverbs 22:20-21

The "unction" we have from the Holy One of Israel is an anointing, and this word indicates smearing or rubbing-in of something. The something being rubbed into us is the divine nature of the Lord Jesus Christ! We are being smeared with His mind and His abilities. There are many, many testimonies of how God brings to our minds the things we need to know, whether it's for a specific test answer or just for life in general. He's very generous with His mind.

In and through God, we know all things. He has given us the answers, the excellent things, so that we can have the right answers to give to others. We're not stupid! Having the mind of Christ means we can use His mind and not have to depend on our own. Praise God!

Rejection says: "I'm a slow learner."

God says: *"The heart of the wise teacheth his mouth, and addeth learning to his lips"* (Proverbs 16:23).

According to the Word, it is God's wisdom that teaches me, and so I have no problem in that area. I am not a slow learner.

Rejection says: "I have a handicap that prevents me, or a lack of coordination that prevents me, or a sickness, or a lack of organizational skills, or a lack of training." (I am inadequate in some way, and I just can't do it.)

God says: *"I can do all things through Christ which strengtheneth me"* (Philippians 4:13).

> Ye have not chosen me, but I have chosen
> you, and ordained you, that ye should go and
> bring forth fruit, and that your fruit should

remain: that whatsoever ye shall ask of the
Father in my name, he may give it you.

John 15:16

Grace and peace be multiplied unto you
through the knowledge of God, and of Jesus
our Lord, According as his divine power hath
given unto us all things that pertain unto
life and godliness, through the knowledge of
him that hath called us to glory and virtue.

2 Peter 1:2-3

*"O taste and see that the LORD is good: blessed is the
man that trusteth in him. O fear the LORD, ye his saints: for
there is no want to them that fear him"* (Psalm 34:8-9).

God has given us all things. There is nothing
lacking to us; there is nothing to prevent us. We are
ordained of God, not man. It is God who qualifies us,
not man. And it is God who promotes us and sets us
in heavenly places with Christ Jesus, where He can
pour us out onto and into the world to be a blessing.
We are His creation, created for good works and good
fruit. We were not created to sit around and listen to
rejection tell us we can't. Hallelujah!

*"For we are his workmanship, created in Christ Jesus unto
good works, which God hath before ordained that we should
walk in them"* (Ephesians 2:10).

Let's stop rejecting ourselves and the opportunities God presents to us to advance His kingdom, shall we? Let's stop rejecting our brothers and sisters as a defense against being hurt by their rejection. Let's stop listening to the words of rejection from inside our own heads, imagining worthless thoughts that carry us into misery. Let's stop labeling ourselves and others in negative ways. Let's stop receiving words of rejection from others—family and friends and coworkers and even strangers—as the truth.

It's time to reject rejection and learn to develop and enjoy the talents and abilities the Lord has given us.

It's time to reject rejection and learn to live in the love and acceptance of our Father in heaven.

Father God, thank You for revealing so clearly the words of the spirit of rejection. Help me recognize them, not only when they come from the lips of others, but also when they issue from my own lips. I do not want to curse myself or any of Your children by agreeing with rejection and speaking its language. Make me aware of my thoughts, Lord, and the words of rejection that enter my imagination and have a conversation with me so that I can reject rejection. I repent to You, Father, for taking the opinions of man over Your opinion, for accepting the word of another instead of Your word, and for allowing rejection to cause me confusion and heartache. I repent for participating with spirits of rejection and speaking their words to reject others and myself. I ask

You to help me remove the labels that rejection has put on me and restore me to the wonderful person You created me to be so that I can do good works with a pure heart and bring forth good fruit. I declare I will no longer immerse myself in an identity crisis brought on by rejection. I will be defined only by You, Lord. I break all agreement with spirits of rejection from my past and my present. I forgive and release into Your hand all my ancestors who opened the door for spirits of rejection to inhabit my thoughts and mess up my life. I forgive and release all who have rejected me in any way, mother and father, sisters and brothers, friends, spouses, coworkers and acquaintances, and any other person. I forgive them for their words, actions, and attitudes of rejection toward me, and I release them from responsibility for any curse that may have attached itself to me. I take all curses of rejection and give them to the Lord Jesus Christ, who is my curse-bearer. Thank You, Father, for freeing me now from all spirits of rejection. In the name of Jesus. Amen.

Identifying and Overcoming Envy, Jealousy, and Covetousness

"Wrath is cruel, and anger is outrageous;
but who is able to stand before envy?"

Proverbs 27:4

"For jealousy is the rage of a man: therefore
he will not spare in the day of vengeance."

Proverbs 6:34

"For this ye know, that no whoremonger,
nor unclean person, nor covetous man, who
is an idolater, hath any inheritance in the
kingdom of Christ and of God."

Ephesians 5:5

We just read about words and phrases typically used by spirits of rejection and the Word of God that counters each category of attack, be it the assassination of character, appearance, or abilities. Now we're going to do the same thing, focusing on spirits of envy, jealousy, and covetousness. Because these demonic powers are often rooted in other spirits and sprout up from them as super-evil fruits, we'll also be looking at the roots. For instance, spirits of pride, rebellion, bitterness, and control can be fertile soil for fruits of envy, jealousy, and covetousness to grow and manifest in our lives. So this will prove to be a good lesson in how evil spirits complement each other and often work together to accomplish their common goal of devastation in our lives.

It is helpful to define the nature of envy, jealousy, and covetousness. There are subtle differences in these three spirits, especially in the way they manifest and in the words they say. Basically, envy is a feeling of discontentment or ill will because of another's advantage, possessions, or blessings. The devil makes us think we are the ones who deserve and should rightly have the thing another person has, whatever it is. Envy works in all areas: the tangible, such as a new car gotten by your friend or neighbor when you are the one who really needs a new car, and the intangible, such as the friend who is pregnant for the second or third time, and you still don't have any children.

The primary words of envy are: "It's not fair."

When we refuse to participate with the voice that says, "It's not fair!" we end up with a wonderful reward, peace in our souls. Not only will we no longer be replaying the envious situation over and over again in our minds, but also, we will not feel the negative emotions that can cause strife and contention or anger and depression to manifest through us. There is even more to the blessing than peace in our souls because refusing to be envious when the opportunity presents itself is one of the things to which God can respond. We know God does not respond to envy and tells us clearly not to enter into agreement with this spirit.

"Be not thou envious against evil men, neither desire to be with them. For their heart studieth destruction, and their lips talk of mischief" (Proverbs 24:1-2).

"Fret not thyself because of evil men, neither be thou envious at the wicked; For there shall be no reward to the evil man; the candle of the wicked shall be put out" (Proverbs 24:19-20).

According to these scriptures, God's only response to envy is to consider it wicked, which it is, and to snuff it out. But what happens when a person does not participate with envy when given the opportunity? We can give you a great example from a situation and person we know personally. We have a good friend who is saved but definitely not walking with the Lord. He is an environmental engineer who designs and installs all sorts of industrial equipment, from kitchen hoods and ventilation in restaurants to air pollution and dust control systems for manufacturers. We all enjoy having an occasional lunch at a little hole-in-the-wall Deli tucked away in a residential neighborhood across town. Recently, the owners decided to expand their facility and put in fryers, which require hoods and ventilation systems. Our friend gave them a bid on doing the installation work.

As a good customer and also a well-seasoned expert in his field, he was pretty certain he'd get the job; and by the way, he really needed it because his business had been slow. But the owners of our favorite Deli decided to go with another company. At first, our friend was upset; actually, we were all a little upset, but then one day, not long after he lost the job, our friend was at our home for dinner. He mentioned that he'd been to the Deli and how they had expanded and how the menu was bigger, and the fried shrimp were so good and so on. I commented that I was surprised he'd still be eating there after they gave the work to someone else to do. His response was, "I saw what they got, and they did the right thing. The way the other company put it together was a better idea than I gave them, and they got it all for less." That is an attitude of humility.

Rather than stewing about missing the job and the money and not being respected for his many years in the business and his great engineering expertise, this man was able to step back and take an objective look, not one based on pride or emotions, or "It's not fair." He recognized the best thing for his friends at the Deli and was able to rejoice with them in having it successfully finished. He was at peace with what happened. Now here's the rest of the story.

Because of the slowdown in his industry and the economic condition of our area at the time, our friend had fallen behind in his shop rent. He got an eviction notice and was told to vacate the shop in thirty days and immediately pay $7,000 in back rent. This would have been impossible on both counts, so he contacted the property manager, who contacted the owner, and they all had a meeting. Our friend explained that because of the amount of heavy equipment he had and other materials, it would take him three months to move out and that he could pay them $1,000 every three weeks but was unable to clear the debt any other way. In an unprecedented move, the owner had the manager draw up an agreement in which our friend would agree to clear the property lot of some old cars and stuff that had been left there by the previous tenant, pay the $1,000 every three weeks for the three months (which amounted to normal rent), and the owner agreed to forego the back rent altogether. In other words, our friend was given a $7,000 break, much more than he would have made on the Deli kitchen deal. It was like putting money in his pocket. I have to believe that was God. The Lord looked on his heart and his attitude of humility and responded as only God can.

There was no pride in our friend's assessment of the situation, and so envy did not have that soil in which to take root. This doesn't mean that the spirit of envy didn't talk to him. It did! He was disappointed that his company wasn't selected to do the work. Envy said, "They should have taken my bid and let me do this job. I eat here a lot, and I have the experience to do it right. It's not fair."

Notice once again, envy and other evil spirits speak to us in the first person. Hell wants us to think its evil thoughts are our own thoughts. Remember, we can't separate ourselves from ourselves! So whenever we think, "It's not fair," we need to examine where that thought is coming from. Chances are good that envy is working.

When we think, "It's not fair!" let's remember God can, and will, equal the playing field when we respond to His ability and take on His nature of humility. "It's not fair" is the word of envy and should never be a phrase we adopt as truth because God's truth is greater, higher, and eternal. "It's not fair" is a temporary condition that will cause us misery, heartache, and even health issues if we dwell in it. The Word of God warns that participating with envy has a devastating result.

"For wrath killeth the foolish man, and envy slayeth the silly one" (Job 5:2).

"A sound heart is the life of the flesh: but envy the rottenness of the bones" (Proverbs 14:30).

In these verses, we can see the result of envy. Envy makes us physically ill and can even kill us. This is not to mention the mental devastation and emotional upheaval we can experience from the words and work of this spirit in our lives. And neither does it take into account the actions we are enticed to perform, which can leave us in deep trouble. These two verses simply address the physical. Envy makes us ill, and we can die as a result of it. That's a harsh word, but a good word because when we know the result is not good, we will more likely choose to refuse to participate with envy. The immune system is based in the bones, and if the bones are rotten, then the immune system is compromised. Envy is the rottenness of the bones. God said it. I believe it. If we want a healthy immune system, which comes as a direct result of having healthy bones, then we must not fall victim to the spirit of envy.

Next, we need to define and explain a little about jealousy. Jealousy manifests in a feeling of being compelled to hold on to something. You become very careful of the thing and guard it; if the object of your jealousy is a person, you won't want to let the person out of your sight. If the object of your jealousy is a possession, you won't want anyone else to touch it or use it. Jealousy guards a thing zealously, does not tolerate rivals, and can easily make an idol out of a material object, a person, or a place. Like envy, jealousy works in both tangible and intangible areas.

The primary words of jealousy are: "It's mine."

One of the most interesting things we noted about jealousy in the Bible is that jealousy is an emotion primarily reserved for God.

"For thou shalt worship no other god: for the LORD, whose name is Jealous, is a jealous God" (Exodus 34:14).

"For the LORD thy God is a consuming fire, even a jealous God" (Deuteronomy 4:24).

"God is jealous, and the LORD revengeth; the LORD revengeth, and is furious; the LORD will take vengeance on his adversaries, and he reserveth wrath for his enemies" (Nahum 1:2).

"Therefore thus saith the Lord GOD; Now will I bring again the captivity of Jacob, and have mercy upon the

whole house of Israel, and will be jealous for my holy name" (Ezekiel 39:25).

We want to say here that it is possible to experience the same emotion of jealousy in a godly way, although most feelings of jealousy that enter our thoughts and manifest in actions are ungodly. This kind of jealousy is not an emotion at all; it is an evil spirit at work. Also, even when the jealousy is godly jealousy, like a mother's protection over her young children, very few of us can express jealousy in a godly way that will leave us unscathed. Expressing jealousy, even if the feeling itself is godly and right, can bring devastation into our lives.

The third spirit of this trifold cord of evil is covetousness. Covetousness manifests itself as a longing for something in the wrong way, greed or avarice.

The primary words of covetousness are: "I want more."

When a spirit of covetousness is operating, we are never really satisfied, no matter how much we have or acquire. And again, covetousness can be at work in the tangible and the intangible. For example, a collector of bean bags will want more and more and more bean bags until every inch of his house is covered in them and then get a bigger house to accommodate his ever-growing collection. There will never be enough bean bags for him. Covetousness can also manifest in intangible ways, such as moving from relationship to relationship for the thrill of "first times" or using more and more or different kinds of drugs for the excitement and anticipation of how they might make you feel. Covetousness and addiction are not the same spirit, but they can certainly work together. Jesus warned of covetousness.

"And he said unto them, Take heed, and beware of covetousness: for a man's life consisteth not in the abundance of the things which he possesseth" (Luke 12:15).

Having stuff is not what life is about. Advancing the kingdom of God is what life is all about! It's not about me and what I have; it's about the Lord and what He has for me. Covetousness, like envy and jealousy, can also lead a person into idolatry and addiction. We become consumed in acquiring, so the very act of acquiring becomes addictive. Then we begin to bow the knee to the thing of our focus, whether it's money, or shoes, or books with red covers. Coveting puts our focus on the thing we desire and takes it off of God. We think about and plan for the next acquisition, whatever it is, and obtaining the next one only leaves us longing for the one after that; we're never satisfied. But the Bible says we are to be content with what we have.

Let your conversation [that's your character,
the style or mode of your life] be without
covetousness; and be content with such
things as ye have: for he hath said, I will
never leave thee, nor forsake thee.

Hebrews 13:5

In other words, all we need is God. If we are first
seeking His kingdom and His righteousness, the Word
assures us that all other things will be added to our
lives. Our covetousness must be restricted to the gifts
of God and what He wants us to have for His purposes.
Coveting the gifts of God, specifically, the best gift, is
the only proper covetousness. The problem seems to
be that we've been coveting the wrong things, doesn't
it? We may even have been taught that it's okay to
want more and more and more and that it's God's job
to give it to us! We like to remind God, "You said You'd
give me the desires of my heart, God, and I want more!
More of this, more of that, more, more-more!"

A friend shared a revelation on that scripture about
the desires of the heart. He was asking the Lord about
it, reminding Him, as we've all done, "What about this,
Lord? You said You'd give me the desires of my heart."
And he heard God clearly say, "If you will learn to
desire the things I want you to have, My faith will work
for you 100 percent of the time."

God showed him the connection between the desires of the heart and faith. You see, covetousness is a subtle form of unbelief. When we have to have more and more and more, it's simply evidence that we are not trusting God. We end up striving in the world to maintain a level that is usually much lower than God has for us.

"When ye go, ye shall come unto a people secure, and to a large land: for God hath given it into your hands; a place where there is no want of any thing that is in the earth" (Judges 18:10).

"He brought me forth also into a large place; he delivered me, because he delighted in me" (Psalm 18:19).

When we are covetous, it says we don't really trust the Lord to provide for us. We become very busy or even frantic in our attempts to fill a void or stuff a storehouse we think we might need to carry us through hard times. We don't truly grasp it is God that carries us through at all times. Stuff can't do it. Our lifestyle should reflect the stuff of our God, not that stuff is our god.

There's one more thing to say about covetousness, and perhaps this is the most important thing to remember in our Christian walk. Being covetous robs us of authority. The Word is clear: "Nor thieves, nor covetous, nor drunkards, nor revilers, nor extortioners, shall inherit the kingdom of God" (1 Corinthians 6:10).

Kingdom authority is reserved for those who are content with what they have, for those who seek first the kingdom of God and His righteousness, for those who understand that abundance of possessions is not a criteria God uses to choose His leaders, and for those who trust the Lord to provide whatever is needed. Kingdom authority is for those who recognize that provision is for the vision, and the vision must be in line with heaven to advance the purposes of God and not the agenda of "self."

There are seven things named in Proverbs 6, which are described as abominable to the Lord. All of these actions and attitudes can result from participation with evil spirits of envy, jealousy, or covetousness. As we continue, we will also look more specifically at the language of spirits in which envy, jealousy, and covetousness are rooted and those that most frequently team up together to mess with our lives and happiness.

> These six things doth the LORD hate: yea, seven are an abomination unto him: A proud look, a lying tongue, and hands that shed innocent blood, An heart that deviseth wicked imaginations, feet that be swift in

running to mischief, A false witness that speaketh lies, and he that soweth discord among brethren.

Proverbs 6:16-19

Pride is first on this list. Pride manufactures fuel for envy: "I can do it better; I should have been the one chosen. It's not fair because I deserve it, and he doesn't."

The second thing, a lying tongue, is promoted by all three spirits. We lie with our lips when we speak to subvert or overthrow another person because of envy. There are other ways lying is promoted. If your dad is very jealous of his car, and you accidentally scratched it, dragging the trash can out of the garage to the street, you would be tempted to say you didn't know how it happened. I remember once when I was going shopping and my husband said, "Don't buy one more purple thing," but I did. I bought this great patterned, purple shirt and sneaked it into the house and hid it. When I wore it the first time, he asked, "Is that new?" Guess what I said. I said no. I reasoned that technically it wasn't a lie because I had the shirt for more than a week before I wore it.

Jealousy in relationships can result in the next action on the list, which is violent behavior. This is expressed as "hands that shed innocent blood." The

Word says, "Jealousy is the rage of a man" (Proverbs 6:34). It can lead to anger and violence, and even murder. The Word says Jesus was delivered up by the Pharisees and chief priests to be crucified because of envy.

Next, a heart that devises wicked imaginations can come into play with any of the three spirits. My daughter, who was herself a "pageant mom" of a very talented daughter, was telling us pageant stories during a Miss America event we were viewing, and she said that the girls have to guard their dresses and glitzy things so that some envious competitor doesn't flush them in the toilet or damage them in other ways. Jealousy can cause us to imagine our husband in the arms of another woman if he's late coming home from work. And covetousness will create all sorts of clever ways for us to get what we want, no matter what the cost may be to others.

Feet that are "swift in running to mischief" are often a result of allowing envy or jealousy to rise up so that we retaliate against people, companies, or whatever. People have been known to lose their jobs because they were envious of the boss or a coworker and made a photocopy of some private body part to leave on his desk as an expression of scorn. Wanting more and more, or coveting what another has, can lead to stealing and other even worse actions of mischief and evil.

Being a false witness is a very common manifestation of envy and jealousy. We don't like the person because he has something we don't have, so we lie to get him in trouble and possibly lose the possession or position of which we are envious. "If I can't have it, you can't either!" Or, in the case of jealousy, we might bring false accusations against the ones we claim to love most because jealousy makes us unable to trust them.

Last on the list, we have "sowing discord among the brethren." If we're envious of leadership, we may attempt to divide a group and draw people to "our side" or pit our coworkers against the boss, that kind of thing. Both jealousy and covetousness will also cause harmony to be broken. There is no peace where these spirits are at work.

"For where envying and strife is, there is confusion and every evil work" (James 3:16).

Please notice that envy and strife open the door for every evil work. When we hear the words of envy, jealousy, and covetousness, we need to say no and refuse to listen, agree, or participate with any of them. Take these words out of your thoughts and out of your vocabulary:

"It's not fair."

"It's mine."

"I want more!"

Father God, thank You for freeing me of attitudes and actions brought on by spirits of envy, jealousy, and covetousness. Thank You for making it clear that I can separate myself from these spirits, and give me the courage to do it! Make me aware, Lord, when I begin to think, "It's not fair," that You are the Just Judge and You will right all wrongs against me. Give me more of Your divine nature of love and humility, Father, so I can put down envy and never pick it up, and so that You can promote me.

Make me aware, Lord, when I begin to think, "It's mine," that there is nothing I possess that did not come from You and that the only things I will ever truly be able to keep are the things I am willing to give up. Give me more of Your divine generosity and compassion, Father, so that I can put down ungodly jealousy and walk in Your power.

Make me aware, Lord, when I begin to think, "I want more," that You are my Provider and my provision and Your name is Jehovah-Jireh, God will see to it. Help me trust that You will make sure I have everything I need to advance Your kingdom on the earth and fulfill my destiny in You, and that's the only thing that has eternal value. Stuff isn't important, and it's not a criterion with You. Give me a greater measure of Your faith, Lord, so I can put down covetousness and receive all You have for me.

In the name of Jesus, I break all agreement now with spirits of envy, jealousy, and covetousness and all evil spirits associated or connected to them. I break agreement with: competition, discontent, pride, fear, not trusting

God, idolatry, superiority, critical spirits, possessiveness, strife, selfish ambition, comparison, control, rivalry, gossip, bitterness, unforgiveness, resentment, retaliation, anger, hatred, violence, and murder. I take the sword of the spirit of God and sever all generational cords of iniquity and evil soul ties that held these things in place in my life, and I command every familiar spirit from the generations and every spirit guide associated with anything I have named to leave me, in the name of Jesus and by the power of the Holy Spirit. Father, in every place where an unclean spirit has left, I ask to be filled with every fruit of Your Holy Spirit: love, joy, peace, patience, faith, meekness, goodness, gentleness, and self-control. Fill me up, Lord! I declare the blood of the Lord Jesus Christ is all-powerful and effective to keep me from these evils. Amen.

Identifying and Overcoming Rebellion

"An evil man seeketh only rebellion: there-fore a cruel messenger shall be sent against him."

Proverbs 17:11

We hear the voice of the enemy in our thoughts and through words that are spoken to us or about us by others. To avoid falling victim to a demonic voice, we need to know who's speaking. So far, we have revealed some of the words and phrases typically used by spirits of rejection, envy, jealousy, and covetousness and how to counter the attacks of the enemy in those areas by using God's Word and authority. We explained briefly that we need to examine the roots, as well as eliminate the fruits of the enemy. For example, if spirits of envy or jealousy or covetousness continue to come back to plague us and throw us off track, perhaps we have not recognized and dealt with one or more root spirits.

For instance, spirits of pride, rebellion, bitterness, and control can be fertile soil for fruits of envy, jealousy, and covetousness to grow and manifest in our lives. Roots and fruit work the same way in the spirit as they do in the natural. Say you have a pear tree, and you hate pears. The tree produces fruit, and what fruit does it produce? Pears. So you pluck off all the pears and throw them out. Now you're happy until the next season, and once again, your pear tree produces fruit. Now you're really angry, and so you once again get rid of all the pears and even cut the branches off the tree. All you've accomplished is a pruning process that will cause that pear tree to put on even more fruit next season. If you want to get rid of pears in your life, you have to cut through the root of the tree. If rebellion, pride, control, or bitterness grows the fruit of envy or jealousy or covetousness, getting rid of its fruit or branches is not enough to solve the problem. You must take the ax to the root of the tree!

"And now also the axe is laid unto the root of the trees: therefore every tree which bringeth not forth good fruit is hewn down, and cast into the fire" (Matthew 3:10).

Many times, evil spirits work together to accomplish a common goal of devastation and destruction. For example, we understand how the favorite words of envy, "It's not fair," can easily lead us into rebellion. "Well, it wasn't fair when I had to babysit instead of going out with my friends, so the next time I get out, I'm going to stay out as long as I want to!"

On the flip side of that coin, we have rebellious behavior triggering envy in someone else. "Wow, Johnny gets away with everything, and I can't. I wish I was like Johnny. He does whatever he wants to." Now both spirits are working in concert with each other and messing up one life after another after another.

So what is rebellion? Our Webster's dictionary gives us these definitions:

1. an act or state of armed, open resistance to authority, government, etc.;
2. a defiance of, or opposition to any control;
3. a rebelling.[2]

From these definitions, it seems safe to say that rebellion is willful disobedience. God is, or should be, the dominant authority in our lives. If we do not follow what He says in His Word, we are rebellious. In some area or another, every one of us is rebellious against God. If you disagree, that's okay, but consider this:

God's will is for us to respect authority. Jesus Christ Himself obeyed the law of the land and the authority of His Father. If you drive faster than the speed limit, you are willfully disobeying the law, and you're rebellious. If your boss called a business meeting for two o'clock, and you come in at 2:05, you're rebellious. You've willfully disobeyed the authority of your boss. That may sound harsh, but it's a true word.

While we're defining rebellion, we need to take a look at the Hebrew words and their basic meanings. We found this very interesting because the first time the word "rebellion" is used in Scripture, it means "bitterness," and in the second use of the word "rebellion," it means "to be or make bitter, to rebel or resist, to provoke."[3] Both these uses of the word "rebellion" are in Deuteronomy 31.

> And it came to pass, when Moses had made an end of writing the words of this law in a book, until they were finished, That Moses commanded the Levites, which bare the ark of the covenant of the LORD, saying, Take this book of the law, and put it in the side of the ark of the covenant of the LORD your God, that it may be there for a witness against thee. For I know thy rebellion, and thy stiff neck: behold, while I am yet alive

with you this day, ye have been rebellious
against the LORD; and how much more after
my death?

Deuteronomy 31:24-27

Moses told the people they were bitter and
stubborn, and even in his presence, they were prone to
provoke God. He wanted them to have a solid copy of
their instructions from God because he thought they
would become even more resistant to the Lord after
he was gone from them. He believed the people would
need a reminder of the law of God. We're the same way
because we listen to the voice of rebellion, just as the
Israelites did, and we, too, have been left a reminder of
God's law of love; it is the Bible.

We all know how the Israelites willfully disobeyed
God and the many times Moses interceded for them.
One time Moses stood in the gap for the people and
said, "Kill me instead, Lord. Take my life and spare
these people." Another time, he used a different tactic
and said, "Forgive them, Lord, because if You kill 'em,
it'll only make You look bad."

In other passages of Scripture, the word "rebellion"
means "rebellion, or revolt, or apostasy."[4] If there
were a dictionary of demonology, the word "rebellion"
would mean destruction, as would all the rest of
the words in that dictionary. The dictionary of

87

demonology doesn't really exist, as far as we know. But if it did, there would be lots of words but only one primary definition, and that is "destruction." The destruction can be any number of things and in any aspect of life. The destruction of the demonic goes from poverty to sickness to death, to ruin, and every other evil circumstance.

So what does rebellion look like? It's simple: anything that challenges authority is rebellion. Talking back (yes, contention is a form of rebellion), refusing to obey (yes, disobedience is a form of rebellion), or saying one thing and doing another (yes, hypocrisy is a form of rebellion). Whatever challenges authority, by word or deed, is rebellion.

Rebellion says: "Who do you think you are?" "Who put you in charge?"

> Now Korah, the son of Izhar, the son of
> Kohath, the son of Levi, and Dathan and
> Abiram, the sons of Eliab, and On, the son
> of Peleth, sons of Reuben, took men: And
> they rose up before Moses, with certain
> of the children of Israel, two hundred and
> fifty princes of the assembly, famous in
> the congregation, men of renown: And
> they gathered themselves together against
> Moses and against Aaron, and said unto

them, Ye take too much upon you, seeing
all the congregation are holy, every one
of them, and the LORD is among them:
wherefore then lift ye up yourselves above
the congregation of the LORD?

Numbers 16:1-3

Here we see rebellion as bitterness, causing envy and (as we shall soon see) resulting in destruction. Korah had bitterness and revolted against the authority God had placed over him. He said, "Moses, we are every bit as good as you are and as deserving as you are, and we can lead as well as you do. So, who do you think you are, telling us what to do all the time? Who put you in charge?" If you recall, the Pharisees challenged Jesus the same way when they said, "By what authority do you do these things?" In other words, "Who put you in charge?"

And when Moses heard it, he fell upon his
face: And he spake unto Korah and unto all
his company, saying, Even to morrow the
LORD will shew who are his, and who is holy;
and will cause him to come near unto him:
even him whom he hath chosen will he cause
to come near unto him. This do; Take you
censers, Korah, and all his company; And put

fire therein, and put incense in them before the LORD to morrow: and it shall be that the man whom the LORD doth choose, he shall be holy: ye take too much upon you, ye sons of Levi. And Moses said unto Korah, Hear, I pray you, ye sons of Levi: Seemeth it but a small thing unto you, that the God of Israel hath separated you from the congregation of Israel, to bring you near to himself to do the service of the tabernacle of the LORD, and to stand before the congregation to minister unto them? And he hath brought thee near to him, and all thy brethren the sons of Levi with thee: and seek ye the priesthood also? For which cause both thou and all thy company are gathered together against the LORD: and what is Aaron, that ye murmur against him?

Numbers 16:4-11

In these verses, Moses answers Korah, but only after consulting God. Notice that Moses did not try to defend himself or his position. Instead, he immediately "fell on his face." This is the opposite of rebellion; it is submission. The Lord told Moses, "You don't have to answer these guys. Tell them to come back tomorrow, and I'll answer them Myself!" It seems pretty obvious that Moses knew God's answer would not be beneficial to Korah because he made an appeal to the group. "Why would you do this? Don't you know how serious and important you are to the Lord in what He appointed you to do? Why do you want to take over everything and promote yourselves? Who are we that you should murmur against us?" In his response to Korah's rebellion against him and against God, Moses showed both submission to God and humility toward his fellowman. No wonder God had put Moses in charge!

> And Moses sent to call Dathan and Abiram, the sons of Eliab: which said, We will not come up: Is it a small thing that thou hast brought us up out of a land that floweth with milk and honey, to kill us in the wilderness, except thou make thyself altogether a prince over us? Moreover thou hast not brought us into a land that floweth with milk and honey, or given us inheritance of fields and vineyards: wilt thou put out the eyes of these men? we will not come up.
>
> Numbers 16:12-14

Here we see rebellion speak a different word, yet still challenging authority.

Rebellion says: "I will not!"

Also, notice this: "I will not!" is usually followed by an accusation. Dathan and Abiram said, "We will not come up, and here's why. Nothing is important to you but you: you want to be in control, and that's all that matters. You don't care if we all die, you've not fulfilled a single promise, and now you want us to come over there so you can blind us."

> And Moses was very wroth, and said unto
> the LORD, Respect not thou their offering:
> I have not taken one ass from them, neither
> have I hurt one of them. And Moses said
> unto Korah, Be thou and all thy company
> before the LORD, thou, and they, and Aaron,
> to morrow: And take every man his censer,
> and put incense in them, and bring ye
> before the LORD every man his censer, two
> hundred and fifty censers; thou also, and
> Aaron, each of you his censer. And they took
> every man his censer, and put fire in them,
> and laid incense thereon, and stood in the
> door of the tabernacle of the congregation
> with Moses and Aaron. And Korah gathered
> all the congregation against them unto the
> door of the tabernacle of the congregation:
> and the glory of the LORD appeared unto all

the congregation. And the LORD spake unto
Moses and unto Aaron, saying, Separate
yourselves from among this congregation,
that I may consume them in a moment. And
they fell upon their faces, and said, O God,
the God of the spirits of all flesh, shall one
man sin, and wilt thou be wroth with all the
congregation?

Numbers 16:15-22

Even Moses had his breaking point, and he reached
it when Dathan and Abiram rebelled openly in a
display of willful disobedience. Moses said to God,
"Lord, don't even accept their sacrifice. They're lying
about me." He was angry. So, Moses told Korah to
come to the tabernacle the next day, and God would
answer his complaint. When the rebellious men
showed up, God told Moses and Aaron, "Stand back!
I'm going to bring these people to an end." Once again,
Moses interceded on behalf of Israel. "God, surely You
won't kill all the people just for a few bad apples!" And
once again, God listened to the plea of Moses and gave
him a new directive, telling him he could warn the
people and give them time to step away from those
who were rebellious.

And the LORD spake unto Moses, saying,
Speak unto the congregation, saying, Get
you up from about the tabernacle of Korah,
Dathan, and Abiram. And Moses rose up
and went unto Dathan and Abiram; and the
elders of Israel followed him. And he spake
unto the congregation, saying, Depart, I pray
you, from the tents of these wicked men, and
touch nothing of theirs, lest ye be consumed
in all their sins.

Numbers 16:23-26

This is a really good lesson to learn. When godly people in authority tell us not to become close to or remain close to rebellious people, we need to heed their advice. Associational sin carries the same, or a very similar, earthly consequence as is sure to come upon the one who sins. Rebellion carries with it destruction, and it often holds envy, jealousy, and covetousness in place. In this account in the book of Numbers, the people listened, and they moved away from Korah and Dathan and Abiram. Moses then pronounced the consequence of the sin of rebellion against authority. He said, "Listen up. This is what the Lord sent me to tell you. If it happens any other way, then the Lord didn't send me, but if it happens as I say, then know it's the Lord that does it, not me. God doesn't like rebellion. It provokes Him."

> So they gat up from the tabernacle of Korah,
> Dathan, and Abiram, on every side: and
> Dathan and Abiram came out, and stood
> in the door of their tents, and their wives,
> and their sons, and their little children. And
> Moses said, Hereby ye shall know that the
> LORD hath sent me to do all these works;
> for I have not done them of mine own mind.
> If these men die the common death of all
> men, or if they be visited after the visitation
> of all men; then the LORD hath not sent me.
> But if the LORD make a new thing, and the
> earth open her mouth, and swallow them
> up, with all that appertain unto them, and
> they go down quick into the pit; then ye shall
> understand that these men have provoked
> the LORD.
>
> Numbers 16:27

And I think most of us know the rest of the story.

> And it came to pass, as he had made an end
> of speaking all these words, that the ground
> clave asunder that was under them: And the

earth opened her mouth, and swallowed
them up, and their houses, and all the men
that appertained unto Korah, and all their
goods. They, and all that appertained to
them, went down alive into the pit, and the
earth closed upon them: and they perished
from among the congregation. And all Israel
that were round about them fled at the cry of
them: for they said, Lest the earth swallow us
up also. And there came out a fire from the
LORD, and consumed the two hundred and
fifty men that offered incense.

Numbers 16:31-35

The earth opened up and swallowed Dathan and
Abiram and their families and flocks and possessions,
and Korah's family and flocks and possessions. And
all the men who aligned themselves with Korah,
those who joined the revolt against authority, were
consumed by the fire of God. Rebellion, working in
concert with envy, destroyed several hundred people
that day. Everyone who was close to Dathan, Abiram,
and Korah, including family and friends and servants,
was killed.

They envied Moses also in the camp, and
Aaron the saint of the LORD. The earth

opened and swallowed up Dathan, and
covered the company of Abiram. And a fire
was kindled in their company; the flame
burned up the wicked.

Psalm 106:16-18

The earthly end of these men is certainly a
testimony to the truth of our opening scripture in
Proverbs 17. It clearly shows if we seek rebellion, we
can expect a cruel messenger. There's another very
important point to look at concerning rebellion. The
Word of God compares rebellion to witchcraft. We
tend to think of witchcraft as a really big sin and
rebellion as just a human tendency, but God says they
are the same.

And Samuel said, Hath the LORD as great
delight in burnt offerings and sacrifices, as
in obeying the voice of the LORD? Behold, to
obey is better than sacrifice, and to hearken
than the fat of rams. For rebellion is as the
sin of witchcraft, and stubbornness is as
iniquity and idolatry. Because thou hast
rejected the word of the LORD, he hath also
rejected thee from being king.

1 Samuel 15:22-23

How can rebellion be witchcraft? First of all, each of these spirits is all about control. A person in rebellion usually thinks another person is trying to control him and seeks to control his own life, "I'll do it my way," and a person in witchcraft is trying to gain control over the life of another, "You'll do it my way." Both are perverted and work with a spirit of perversion. Can you see how all these evil things are connected? Perverseness is "twistedness," it is twisted thinking that causes us to speak words that are meant to subvert and overthrow something or someone, usually a greater authority, either spiritually or physically, whatever that authority happens to be. Korah's rebellion was meant to overthrow Moses' position as leader of the nation and Aaron's position as the high priest who ministered to God. Korah's actions and attitude were perverted and serve as a perfect example:

> He loveth transgression that loveth strife: and he that exalteth his gate seeketh destruction. He that hath a froward heart findeth no good: and he that hath a perverse tongue falleth into mischief.
>
> Proverbs 17:19-20

Korah's heart was "froward," which means "distorted, twisted, knotted, false, perverted."[5] In other words, he had warped thinking because there was a root of rebellion in his heart. That root of rebellion grew an evil fruit of envy, which caused him to exalt himself. This self-exaltation, masked in religious self-righteousness, worked with a spirit of perversity to speak out against Moses and Aaron. Korah sought to subvert and overthrow leadership. He wanted control, and by his words, words that can be considered as working witchcraft, Korah drew people to himself. He brought a spirit of division into the camp, and he fell into evil because of his perverse complaint. Rebellion is as the sin of witchcraft and carries the same devastating consequence.

The spirit world is often so entangled in itself, the demons so intertwined in their workings, it can become difficult to distinguish where one leaves off and another takes up. The good news is that God is bigger and greater and more powerful. He is also infinitely and intimately faithful. He is our covenant-keeping God, Jehovah-Jireh, which means "God will see to it." Perhaps you are feeling a little overwhelmed by all this rebellion as a root, envy as a fruit, or is it envy as a root and rebellion as a fruit? Or is it witchcraft or control, and aren't they the same? But wait, rebellion is the same as witchcraft. Does that make rebellion control? And where does perversity come in? What's that about? It can seem rather confusing, but remember that God is not the author of confusion. The devil would like nothing more than for us to get caught up in the semantics of which demon works best with another, and so on. But if we do, it will take our focus off the solution, which is the power of the blood of Christ. Believe me, it doesn't matter whether rebellion supports envy or envy supports rebellion. What matters is that we cut the legs out from under them both! Just deal with it.

There is an aspect of rebellion that those in leadership in the church must very cautiously avoid, and that is the rebellion that comes from speaking for God when God didn't speak. We all want our words to be sweet, but sometimes the Word of the Lord brings a warning, and it isn't all sweet and nice. To make people think they're okay when they aren't, to condone compromise and complacency in God's people, carries a hefty penalty.

Just as it is rebellious for us to judge people and speak words meant to subvert and overthrow another, it is equally rebellious to speak a word of peace when there is no peace. It is rebellious to add our own interpretation to the Word of the Lord in order to make it sound all pretty. It is rebellious to dilute the gospel of the kingdom of God, and it is dangerous as well because we are teaching people a false doctrine. We engage in a doctrine of demons when we give people only what they want to hear and neglect to tell them the truth. This is the aspect of rebellion that is considered apostasy.

Rebellion says: "God's okay with your sin because He loves you."

It's true that God loves you, but it is not true that He's okay with our sin!

> Then said the prophet Jeremiah unto Hananiah the prophet, Hear now, Hananiah; The LORD hath not sent thee; but thou makest this people to trust in a lie. Therefore thus saith the LORD; Behold, I will cast thee from off the face of the earth: this year thou shalt die, because thou hast taught rebellion against the LORD. So Hananiah the prophet died the same year in the seventh month.
>
> Jeremiah 28:15-17

If we are not ready to depart this earth, then when we say, "Thus saith the Lord," we need to know that the Lord really said it. I can't tell you the number of people we've ministered to over the years who have been totally devastated by a "word from the Lord" that the Lord didn't say. Our caution to everyone is this: when someone says, "I have a word from the Lord for you," listen to the word, thank the person for sharing the word with you, and then if it doesn't resonate as true in your spirit, put it on the shelf. Let the Holy Spirit reveal whether it is a true word and also what the word means. Oftentimes, we immediately go into our minds (or into the flesh, which is the nature of Satan, not you) and decide what the word means. Or we take the prophet's interpretation, which may or may not be correct, and immediately run with it, trying to make it happen.

We know a couple who received a word that they were called into full-time ministry. He immediately quit his job and moved his young family to another state where he could attend seminary and be trained for a pastorate. They had young children, were in a strange place with no family support nearby, the money was running out, the mom had to work two jobs, and the kids were being neglected. The whole experience was a stressful, miserable affair. To make matters worse, after he finished school, having put his family through extreme hardship both emotionally and financially, he couldn't get a job. No church would take him. The doors were closed everywhere he turned. By now, they were all so frustrated with God and with each other it was all they could do to hold on to some semblance of sanity. They turned away from God and went back into the world, where they stayed for most of the formative years of their young children. By the time they came back to God, they felt so burned out on everything and so fearful of the prophetic that it took years of healing to restore them to the level of love and worship they knew when they set out to fulfill the word they had been given.

My personal belief is that the word they got was a true word, but just because you get a true word doesn't mean it's a now word. We must learn to allow the Holy Spirit to birth His purpose in us. Doing anything in our own strength is a form of rebellion. Adding to God's Word is rebellion, speaking "thus saith the Lord" when the Lord didn't say is rebellion, and acting on a word, whether it's a true word or a false word, by moving in our own strength to make it happen, without a confirming peace in our hearts, is also rebellion. We've looked at rebellion from a few different views, and I hope you have a better understanding of how rebellion speaks. Once again, the main voice of rebellion says,

"I will not!"

"Who put you in charge?"

"I'll do whatever I please."

"Who do you think you are?" and

"God's okay with our sin."

Break agreement with rebellion in all its forms by praying the following prayer out loud.

Father God, I thank You once again for Your faithfulness in helping me understand the spirit world and separate myself from all evil. Lord, I recognize spirits of rebellion in myself and in my generations, and I declare to You that I will no longer participate with them. I break all agreement with rebellion in every form, and I ask You to forgive me, Father, for every time I spoke words in judgment of those in authority, words that were designed by the enemy to subvert and overthrow my parents, bosses, pastors, friends, accountability partners, or any other person.

I admit the sin of perversity, Lord, and I pull down from the heavenlies all perverse words I have spoken and also the perverse words that have been spoken over me. I ask You to forgive me, Father, for those times I willfully disobeyed You and others in authority over me, times I refused to do my appointed tasks or follow the words of wisdom and direction of those You placed over me as agents for good in my life. Help me, Lord, to remove the words of rebellion from my thoughts and my tongue.

I ask You to forgive me, Father, for questioning the authority and position of Christian leaders and for coveting their position, place, or assignment in the body of Christ. Forgive me for questioning the authority of my bosses or supervisors and for coveting their position, place, or assignment in the workplace.

I ask You to forgive me, Father, for any time I added to a word You gave me or spoke a word and gave it credence by saying it came from You when it really didn't. Lord, I ask Your forgiveness for all these things and for my participation with rebellion. I stand in the gap for my ancestors now, and I forgive them for any time they opened the door for familiar spirits of rebellion to attach themselves to me. I forgive them and release them now from responsibility for any curse that has come down to me. I take those curses and give them to the Lord Jesus Christ, who is my curse-bearer. Thank You, Father, for freeing me of all rebellion, in Jesus' name. Amen.

Identifying and Overcoming Control

"The righteous is more excellent than his neighbour: but the way of the wicked seduceth them."

Proverbs 12:26

Now we're going to look at another spirit that is closely related to envy, jealousy, and covetousness, and that is the spirit of control. Control is a very seducing spirit. It can be a root of envy, jealousy, and covetousness, and we need to decide to separate ourselves from this evil spirit. Roots and fruit work the same way in the spirit as they do in the natural. If a tree is bearing fruit, and the fruit is bitter or useless, then plucking or cutting off the fruit is only going to be a temporary solution. To be rid of the fruit forever, the tree has to be severed from its root. Otherwise, the root system will continue to nurture the tree, and the tree will continue to produce bad fruit.

Before we get into the language of evil spirits of control, we need to explain that control is not always a bad thing or an evil spirit. Having or taking control of a chaotic situation through the authority of God does not mean you have a controlling spirit. Using control in our own lives to keep our bodies healthy, or to overcome a bad habit, is a good thing, not a bad thing. These are situations where authority comes into play, and there is definitely a difference between having authority and being controlling. One denotes true leadership ability and strength of character, and the other shows fear and insecurity. One exhibits a pure heart; the other spews defilement. So, for the sake of clarity, we're going to look at three evil faces of a controlling spirit: domination, intimidation, and manipulation. The spirit of control (in whatever form it takes) is the same as lust in that it benefits "self" at the sacrifice of others. In addition, all these spirits of control—domination, intimidation, and manipulation—can be tied to witchcraft in some way. Witchcraft is the epitome of control and rebellion. Witchcraft in some form or another, with its physical destruction and spiritual defilement, is the end result of control.

The first spirit in the three-strand cord of control is domination. A spirit of domination generally uses power, typically physical power, to overcome and control another person. Many of the wicked kings of Israel ruled through domination. Rehoboam was one, and his words are an example of the language of domination.

Control using domination says: "I control you and will treat you any way I please." "I'm bigger and stronger than you. I can hurt you, and I will hurt you!"

> And the king answered the people roughly, and forsook the old men's counsel that they gave him. And spake to them after the counsel of the young men, saying, My father made your yoke heavy, and I will add to your yoke: my father also chastised you with whips, but I will chastise you with scorpions.
>
> 1 Kings 12:13-14

We can imagine that these words were terrifying to the people who had come before the king seeking relief from the burdens they were already carrying. Domination uses fear as a tactic to get what it wants. People comply with dominating people because they fear the consequences if they don't. We all need to realize that no one can control us without our agreement and that our lives are meant to be placed into the hands of the Lord. We have the choice as to whether or not we yield to an evil spirit of control operating in another person; we only need to recognize what is happening and press into the authority of the kingdom of God within us.

A spirit of domination can squelch the human spirit so that we are unable to break free of bondage to the person or thing that has demonic control over us. This is what was happening to the Israelites in the land of Egypt. Pharaoh so dominated them that they had no hope. He controlled the people with a strong hand of domination, to the extent that when Moses came to give them the good news that God would deliver them, they could not receive the word.

> Wherefore say unto the children of Israel, I am the LORD, and I will bring you out from under the burdens of the Egyptians, and I will rid you out of their bondage, and I will redeem you with a stretched out arm, and with great judgments: And I will take you to me for a people, and I will be to you a God: and ye shall know that I am the LORD your God, which bringeth you out from under the burdens of the Egyptians. And I will bring you in unto the land, concerning the which I

did swear to give it to Abraham, to Isaac, and
to Jacob; and I will give it you for an heritage:
I am the LORD. And Moses spake so unto
the children of Israel: but they hearkened
not unto Moses for anguish of spirit, and for
cruel bondage.

Exodus 6:6-9

Domination is a cruel spirit that has no mercy
on those it dominates, putting them in demonic
subjection from which there seems to be no escape.
The Israelites were under demonic subjection to
Pharaoh. But God delivered them out of his hand. We
need to realize that even in the bleakest times in our
lives, God is listening to our prayers. He will make a
way of escape for us from the control of domination.
When domination crushes our spirits, God is there to
make a way for us.

*"The LORD is nigh unto them that are of a broken heart;
and saveth such as be of a contrite spirit. Many are the
afflictions of the righteous: but the LORD delivereth him out
of them all"* (Psalm 34:18-19).

There are many examples of domination in the
world. It can manifest through anger and become very
violent, leading to physical abuse, rape, and murder.
But a spirit of domination can also act independently
of anger, or it can hook up with sexual perversion.

Most rape is not committed because of anger but comes about from the need to control another person. Most expressions of lust also stem from spirits of control. Some men—and women, too—are sexually aroused by dominating another person or being dominated by another person. The arousal may be considered sexual lust, but in reality, it is a spirit of control manifesting in a sexual way. Using blindfolds, handcuffs, ropes or chains, whips, and other instruments of masochism and bondage in a sexual encounter is not normal, folks. People who have to have such paraphernalia also have a spirit of control, expressing its face of domination.

Basically, the primary words of domination are "I control you and will do with you what I please" and "I will hurt you!" We see this kind of controlling spirit in marriages, in the workplace, and in the church. It should have no place in any of the three.

As for marriage, the Word of God clearly defines godly structure in the home: first, God the Father, then the man, then the woman, then the children. That is the order of authority, not the order of domination. The woman must submit to the man. That does not mean she must cower in fear, but rather, it means she is to agree with his decisions as his helpmate. The man must honor and respect the woman, not dominate and abuse her. When I married, we declared several verses out of Ephesians as a part of our vows, and some of the people in my family were horrified. They claimed I was opening myself up to be a doormat, and they simply could not allow me to vow I would submit to "that man." For those who may be unfamiliar with these verses, they are:

> Wives, submit yourselves unto your own husbands, as unto the Lord. For the husband is the head of the wife, even as Christ is the head of the church: and he is the saviour of the body. Therefore as the church is subject unto Christ, so let the wives be to their own husbands in every thing. Husbands, love your wives, even as Christ also loved the church, and gave himself for it.
>
> Ephesians 5:22-25

My answer to my family was this, "Read it again. I only have to say 'yes' to him; he has to die for me!" And, of course, many people misinterpret the "as unto the Lord" part of submission. It doesn't mean we should think of our husbands the same as we do God and do whatever they say to do. It means the husband is to be a reflection of the Lord so that we, wives, can follow and obey our husbands in total confidence they have only the best in mind for us. Obviously, for my husband and me, following the order given to us in the Word of the living God has proven itself to be in our best interest. It works for us because we realize we are to be a reflection of Christ and His bride, the church. I have no problem submitting to my husband as unto the Lord because he is such a model of Jesus to me. My prayer is that every married couple out there experience and enjoy the same level of love, trust, and harmony we do and go to even greater levels as you each submit to and agree with God.

Control using domination in the workplace and in the church says: "I'm the boss, you're not."

When control is operating in the workplace, there is no give and take and no room for input from others. Whatever the boss says goes, and if you make any attempt to express an opinion, you're considered a troublemaker. You're bucking the system, and you'll find yourself out of a job. No second chances. The boss is always right. This is not leadership. This is demonic subjection. Domination in the workplace can also express itself in sexual harassment.

Domination in the church is similar to that in the workplace. The pastor will not listen to his congregation. He is always right and refuses to hear revelation from anyone else. He has a plan, and he works it. Anyone who questions his authority in anything is beaten down with the familiar rebuke:

"Touch not God's anointed!" A minister in this place is in a very precarious position with God. The Lord is never obligated to uphold any kingdom a man builds for himself. Each one of us is God's anointed, and we all have the same Holy Spirit within us. Because the leaders of a church have certain assignments and responsibilities does not mean they are spiritually superior to anyone in their charge. We are to respect those in positions of leadership but not worship them or feel they are somehow better than we are.

Control using intimidation says: "If you don't comply, this is what's going to happen to you!"

One of the really interesting aspects of intimidation is this: while a person moving in domination is normally fully aware of it, a person moving in intimidation often does not realize they are intimidating to others. So, while we can generally recognize intimidation in others, it becomes very difficult to see it in ourselves. This is not to say we can't, or don't, intentionally intimidate others. We do that because intimidation gives us power over others. It puts us in control. Because of our lust for control, we may find the spirit of intimidation very accommodating and even useful to us in meeting our goals of getting what we want.

Intimidation offers us the ability to control people and situations and turn them to what we think is our advantage. Intentional intimidation is most often expressed in a verbal threat meant to project fear into a person's future. Intimidation is designed to put a wedge of doubt in the door of our faith so that the devil will have an easier time pushing the door in and invading us. This is what was happening to the Israelites in the days of Hezekiah when the army of Assyria came against them.

> Then Rabshakeh stood and cried with a loud voice in the Jews' language, and spake, saying, Hear the word of the great king, the king of Assyria: Thus saith the king, Let not Hezekiah deceive you: for he shall not be able to deliver you out of his hand: Neither let Hezekiah make you trust in the LORD, saying, The LORD will surely deliver us, and this city shall not be delivered into the hand of the king of Assyria. Hearken not to Hezekiah: for thus saith the king of Assyria, Make an agreement with me by a present, and come out to me, and then eat ye every man of his own vine, and every one of his fig tree, and drink ye every one the waters of his cistern: Until I come and take you away to a land like your own land, a land of corn and wine, a land of bread and vineyards, a land

of oil olive and of honey, that ye may live,
and not die: and hearken not unto Hezekiah,
when he persuadeth you, saying, The LORD
will deliver us. Hath any of the gods of the
nations delivered at all his land out of the
hand of the king of Assyria? Where are the
gods of Hamath, and of Arpad? where are the
gods of Sepharvaim, Hena, and Ivah? Have
they delivered Samaria out of mine hand?
Who are they among all the gods of the
countries, that have delivered their country
out of mine hand, that the LORD should
deliver Jerusalem out of mine hand?

2 Kings 18:28-35

Even though Hezekiah was standing firm in the
word of the Lord, the tactic of intimidation was
brought against the people. Rabshakeh "cried with a
loud voice." In other words, he shouted out for all the
people to hear him and spoke in their native language
so they would understand, and he spoke words of
doubt. "Has any god saved other nations? No. Your
God can't save you, either. Give up now and spare
your lives!" This is a good example of intentional
intimidation. All verbal threatening comes from a
spirit of control, usually in the form of intimidation.

In the biblical example given here, the threat was specific: give up or die. Sometimes the "consequence" is left open-ended, which makes intimidation even more terrifying because fear grips our imaginations, and we can think of a hundred scenarios, all going from bad to worse. "Do what I say, or else!" is a voice of intimidation that can leave a person in a sea of horrific visions in his mind. What will happen? We don't know, but we know we'd better comply, or it's sure to be really bad!

On the other hand, there are many times when a person is intimidating, but it is not intentional on his part. In these cases, the spirit of intimidation is usually non-verbal in the person that seems intimidating but very verbal in the thought life of the person who feels intimidated. Lots of people feel intimidated by their bosses, their spouses, their pastors, their friends, or even their children. It causes timidity to rule the personality and can progress to the point where the intimidated person withdraws completely from social interaction. Spirits of intimidation often train us to be man-pleasers rather than God-pleasers. This turns our focus to self-preservation and may cause us to become manipulative, which is the third face of control. Remember, it's all about control. If we feel intimidated, we feel controlled. We don't like feeling controlled, so we begin to use a different form of control: manipulation, to fight back and regain the control we think we've lost. It's all very warped.

Control operating using manipulation says: "It's okay to do this; there is a benefit in it."

We use manipulation to get what we want out of people, even if it is something we know is wrong. This is what the prophet Balaam did in the matter of King Balak of Moab, who had hired Balaam to curse Israel. God did not allow Balaam to curse the Israelites, but Moab had offered Balaam a great reward to do so. This made Balaam want to please Balak, even though he knew better. I think it's interesting that his name, Balaam, means "not of the people." Balaam was a prophet, but his loyalties did not lie with the Lord and the Lord's people. So, although he was not able to curse Israel as the king of Moab wanted him to, Balaam used manipulation to get the Israelites to accept Moabite women into the camp; and thus, the nation mixed the abominations of false gods into their worship. The Israelites fell victim to the manipulation of Balaam, and the result was devastating to the entire camp.

> And Israel abode in Shittim, and the people began to commit whoredom with the daughters of Moab. And they called the people unto the sacrifices of their gods: and the people did eat, and bowed down to

their gods. And Israel joined himself unto
Baalpeor: and the anger of the LORD was
kindled against Israel.

Numbers 25:1-3

As you read the entire account in Numbers 22–24,
you can easily understand what happened. Balaam
left the king of Moab but encouraged the Israelites
to assimilate the culture of that evil nation. This is
an example of our opening scripture in Proverbs 12,
which tells us the way of the wicked seduced them!
This caused the Lord to bring a plague into the camp,
and over 20,000 people died before their sin was
completely removed from the camp by the killing of
every man and woman involved. Numbers 31 explains
that the manipulative words of Balaam were at the
center of the problem.

And Moses was wroth with the officers of
the host, with the captains over thousands,
and captains over hundreds, which came
from the battle. And Moses said unto them,
Have ye saved all the women alive? Behold,
these caused the children of Israel, through
the counsel of Balaam, to commit trespass
against the LORD in the matter of Peor, and

there was a plague among the congregation
of the LORD.

Numbers 31:14-16

The "counsel" of Balaam was a spirit of
manipulation working through his words to corrupt,
subvert, and overthrow the righteousness of God. It
took an act of judgment against evil for the nation of
Israel to be saved from destruction. Still, many people
died in that cleansing process.

We'd like to take a little aside here to explain God's
judgment and show His mercy. God's judgments, even
in the Old Testament, were full of mercy. We tend to
think the God of the Old Testament was not a loving
Father, and we get this idea from the harshness of
punishments prescribed for sin. But think of this:
God is a generational God, and before the cross, there
was no lasting propitiation for sin. There was no way
a generational curse could be broken off a family,
aside from the death of the sinner. If the adulterer
had children, their participation in adultery would be
worse than the parent. The familiar spirit of adultery
would be strengthened as it traversed the generations.
The harsh punishment of death for sin was mercy on
the generations.

Also, according to Scripture, every person who died
before the cross had the opportunity to accept the

saving grace of the Lord Jesus Christ, who descended into hell to take back the keys of death, hell, and the grave; and He introduced Himself to all who were in the place called "paradise," that holding place of righteous souls who died awaiting the Messiah. The word tells us Jesus preached the gospel to those who had died and "took captivity captive." Those sleeping saints left that holding place and ascended with Jesus into the very presence of their loving Father. Hallelujah! They weren't dead, only sleeping.

This bit of revelation should help us all understand the accounts of God's wrath and judgment in the Old Testament. He is angry at sin, not people, and He is the One who took vengeance on it in the only way possible to spare the generations. Now that we are past the cross, we are the ones appointed to take vengeance on the evil spirits that plague God's people. We do that by stepping into the authority of the kingdom of God and allowing the Lord to work through our words as we bind and cast out the sinful spirits within us. Because of the blood of the Lord Jesus Christ, no longer does a person have to physically die to be delivered from evil. We should be shouting praises to God!

There is still a bit to say about the spirit of control operating through manipulation. Women, in particular, are very good at manipulating others, especially men. We learn as little girls how to wrap daddy around our little finger. Because girls are not generally as physically powerful as boys, and because there are still many stereotypes in the classroom, the playground, and the workplace, spirits of manipulation find it easy to inhabit women. We agree with them because they are useful to us. Of course, we don't realize we are agreeing with an evil spirit and participating in a form of witchcraft and lust. We are just doing what we think comes "naturally" to get our way, work around the physical differences in men and women, and overcome the stereotypes.

The real problem comes when we get accustomed to using these spirits of control to get our way about things, and then suddenly, there comes a day when we can no longer control the spirit. The spirit of control begins to control us. That is when we are really out of control. We say and do things, and we have no idea why. We don't want to be the way we are, but we just can't think anymore, and we can't change what's happening to our minds. Mental hospitals are full of women (and men, too) who used a spirit of control until they became so one with it that it took them over, and they found it impossible to separate themselves from it. When we agree with and use a spirit, the devil is very pleased because he knows if we continue to use the spirit, there will come a time when the spirit will take over and begin to use us.

Controlling spirits also include the spirit of Jezebel and spirits of mind control. We're not going into teaching about Jezebel, but we do need to say this: Because a person uses domination, intimidation, or manipulation does not mean he or she is a Jezebel. The Jezebel spirit is much deeper than most other spirits of control, and a main characteristic of Jezebel is this: When she is given the opportunity to repent, she will not. Pride and rebellion are so entrenched in a person who operates in the Jezebel spirit that he or she is unable to see it at all. Jezebel is thoroughly deceived and thoroughly convinced of her superiority and power. She worships herself, considers herself a prophet, and practices spiritual adultery. She knows better than God and puts herself in the place of God. Jesus tells us Jezebel is in the church. Too often, we bow before her, giving her obeisance and believing her word rather than what God has said.

> Notwithstanding I have a few things against
> thee, because thou sufferest that woman
> Jezebel, which calleth herself a prophetess, to
> teach and to seduce my servants to commit
> fornication, and to eat things sacrificed unto

idols. And I gave her space to repent of her fornication; and she repented not.

Revelation 2:20-21

The other thing about Jezebel is this: the spirit of Jezebel cannot operate without the spirit of Ahab. In a church, pastors and leaders who abdicate their responsibilities over the flock or who fail to spend time in the throne room of God's presence are vulnerable to the seductive spirit of Jezebel. Someone operating in this spirit will slide in and take over a key position in the church. She (or he) will endear herself to the pastor and stay very close to him, often acting as the go-between between the pastor and the congregants. Jezebel will be very friendly to everyone and get close to as many of the leaders as possible, finding out everything she can about them and what's happening in the church. He or she will have a finger in everything that goes on. The pastor will think it's wonderful to have this helpmate available to him.

As we described how the Jezebel spirit usually operates in the church setting, many of you probably thought of someone you know. Please be very careful when you label a person a "Jezebel." This is a very serious accusation, and we will be held accountable for our words. If you suspect Jezebel is operating in your church, do not go to the pastor unless you are absolutely certain the Holy Spirit told you to because the pastor will most likely hear accusation. Remember, he is probably under deception. Do not discuss what you think with your friends because that is gossip. Do not approach the person you believe is operating in the Jezebel spirit because that will cause great retaliation against you.

Take your suspicion to the Lord. Bring it before the throne of heaven. Intercede for your pastor and the church, not accusingly but in humility. Speak spiritual strength and discernment for your pastor and seek protection for him. Pull down strongholds of deception and witchcraft. Run to the throne, not the phone! Call forth the spirit of truth to be revealed to leadership. Speak a blessing of truth and humility over the one acting like Jezebel and ask the Lord for His gift of repentance to be given to the acknowledging of the truth. Ask Him to rid the church of all unclean spirits by exposing them to His marvelous light.

Let's add that supplication for our pastors and churches to our prayer and declaration.

Father God, thank You once again for Your marvelous insights into the language of the spirit realm. I declare to You right now that I do not want any spirits of control to be a part of my life. You only, Lord, are the One who controls me. I want to be led by Your Holy Spirit and no other. Neither do I want to control others. Lord, I recognize and repent to You for my part in entertaining spirits of domination, intimidation, and manipulation and for participating with them. Forgive me, Lord, for speaking words of ultimatum or threat. Forgive me for manipulating others so that I could have my own way or get something I wanted.

I break all agreement with spirits of control and renounce them completely. I forgive all my ancestors for any time they opened a door for these evil spirits, or any spirits of mind control, to become a part of my family line. I forgive them and release them from responsibility for any curse that has attached itself to me or my children. I take those curses now and give them to the Lord Jesus because He is my curse-bearer.

I now speak to Satan and all his demons. I put you on notice that I now renounce any and all legal holds or grounds that spirits of mind control may have on me. In the name of Jesus Christ of Nazareth, who "is come in the flesh" (1 John 4:2), I renounce every contact with mind control that I know about and also those I do not know about. Specifically, I renounce any mind control holds or evil soul ties on me from…(mention names of family members, past/present friends, acquaintances, doctors, psychologists, psychiatrists, therapists, bosses, coworkers, psychics, religious leaders, preachers) or any other person.

I also renounce any and all mind control manipulations I may have exercised, knowingly or unknowingly, toward any person.

I now renounce any and all mind control holds or ties from any groups or organizations…(the occult, witchcraft, *new age, karate; transcendental meditation; yoga groups; Jewish mysticism, the kabbala, false Messiah; Sai Baba, ascended masters of the New Age; hypnosis, the military, satanic ritual abuse, Islam, anti-Christ, Santeria, voodoo, cults or churches teaching false doctrines, individual musicians or groups; medical modalities, biofeedback, or medicines). I claim my freedom from all these things in the name of my Lord and Savior Jesus Christ because of His resurrection victory over all the power of the enemy.*

Lord, I ask that You send angels of protection into my church to surround the leadership and that You expose all dark spirits of Jezebel that would destroy my pastor or my church. Visit us with Your spirit of truth, Lord, and tear down any strongholds of deception. In the name of Jesus. Amen.

Identifying and Overcoming Bitterness

Hide me from the secret counsel of the wicked; from the insurrection of the workers of iniquity: Who whet their tongue like a sword, and bend their bows to shoot their arrows, even bitter words.

Psalm 64:2

We've been looking at a grouping of demons that often work together to support each other to accomplish destruction in our lives. We delved into the language of envy, jealousy, and covetousness and said there are four other spirits that help hold these sins in place. It's time to look at bitterness, see what this evil spirit has to say, and learn how to counter its vitriolic words.

We can't really talk about bitterness without mentioning its primary cohorts, unforgiveness and resentment. Roots of bitterness are planted when we listen to the voice of unforgiveness and the voice of resentment. These two give way and open the door for retaliation. Anger and violence then tag along, and pretty soon, we're into hatred, and spirits of murder and self-murder march into our hearts. All these are attached to bitterness, and bitterness works to hold envy and jealousy and covetousness in place in our lives and circumstances. It's all a demonic mess!

While each one of these conditions, or attitudes, unforgiveness, resentment, retaliation, anger, hatred, violence, and murder, is in itself an evil spirit, each one is also a manifestation of a form of bitterness. And we have all experienced every one of them at some time or another in our lives. As we participate in unforgiveness, bitterness grows. As we entertain resentment, bitterness grows. It's the same with the others. There is a progression to bitterness, and it is not pretty.

Unforgiveness says:
"The offense is too big; I cannot forgive him."
"He doesn't deserve to be forgiven."
"If I forgive him, he'll just do it again."
"I'm not ready to forgive him."

These are all voices of unforgiveness that plant and nurture bitterness. Unforgiveness takes occasion to attach itself to us when someone wrongs us or someone we love. If this spirit can get us to agree with its ungodly reasoning, it can keep us out of a personal relationship with God. In the story of the servant who owed his master a great deal of money, the master expected the servant to show the same compassion that had been shown to him.

> Then his lord, after that he had called him, said unto him, O thou wicked servant, I forgave thee all that debt, because thou desiredst me: Shouldest not thou also have had compassion on thy fellowservant, even as I had pity on thee? And his lord was wroth, and delivered him to the tormentors, till he should pay all that was due unto him. So likewise shall my heavenly Father do also unto you, if ye from your hearts forgive not every one his brother their trespasses.
>
> Matthew 18:32-35

God expects something from us, don't you think? He expects us to be like He is, to forgive our brothers and sisters for the offenses they bring against us. Why is that? I believe it's because forgiveness is a spiritual force that destroys the enemy. Forgiving others renders the enemy of our souls totally ineffective in accomplishing his assignments against us. Demonic forces become weaponless in the face of forgiveness. Unforgiveness says the offense is too great. God says: *"Great peace have they which love thy law: and nothing shall offend them"* (Psalm 119:165).

Unforgiveness says the person who brought the offense doesn't deserve to be forgiven. God says we were the same.

> And as for thy nativity, in the day thou wast born thy navel was not cut, neither wast thou washed in water to supple thee; thou wast not salted at all, nor swaddled at all. None eye pitied thee, to do any of these unto thee, to have compassion upon thee; but thou wast cast out in the open field, to the lothing of thy person, in the day that thou wast born. And when I passed by thee, and saw thee polluted in thine own blood, I said unto thee when thou wast in thy blood, Live; yea, I said unto thee when thou wast in thy blood, Live.
>
> Ezekiel 16:4-6

For when we were yet without strength, in
due time Christ died for the ungodly. For
scarcely for a righteous man will one die: yet
peradventure for a good man some would
even dare to die. But God commendeth his
love toward us, in that, while we were yet
sinners, Christ died for us.

Romans 5:6-8

Unforgiveness says if I forgive the offense, it will
happen again. God says:

Then came Peter to him, and said, Lord, how
oft shall my brother sin against me, and I
forgive him? till seven times? Jesus saith
unto him, I say not unto thee, Until seven
times: but, Until seventy times seven.

Matthew 18:21-22

Unforgiveness says I have to be ready, it's not time
yet, the hurt is too fresh. God says:

And when they were come to the place,
which is called Calvary, there they crucified
him, and the malefactors, one on the right
hand, and the other on the left. Then said
Jesus, Father, forgive them; for they know

not what they do. And they parted his
raiment, and cast lots.

Luke 23:33-34

The pain can't be any fresher than that, and yet the
Lord forgave His persecutors. You may want to say,
"Yeah, but that was Jesus." Okay. How about Stephen?
Did he hold unforgiveness until a proper time had
passed?

And they stoned Stephen, calling upon God,
and saying, Lord Jesus, receive my spirit.
And he kneeled down, and cried with a loud
voice, Lord, lay not this sin to their charge.
And when he had said this, he fell asleep.

Acts 7:59-60

Each and every word the spirit of unforgiveness
will bring to prevent us from forgiving an offense is
invalid. Let me say that again. There is no valid reason
not to forgive someone. There is no offense too great,
no person too unworthy, no time too near the offense.
Being "ready" to forgive isn't the issue. Believing God
is capable of handling the situation is the issue. If
you don't believe God is a just judge and will right all
wrongs against you, it will be hard to forgive others.
You will always want to be God and handle it yourself,

thinking you know how things should be. That is
the deception of unforgiveness. Our Father wants to
handle the painful things for us. He wants to heal us,
and He wants to bring us justice. Too often, He cannot
do that because we are holding onto the offense and
won't let go. His advice is, "Use the wisdom from
above, not the wisdom of the world. Be like Jesus and
forgive, no matter what. If you do, I'll take care of the
details."

*"My son, be wise, and make my heart glad, that I may
answer him that reproacheth me"* (Proverbs 27:11).

This verse tells us that when we follow wisdom
(which is Jesus Christ) by forgiving others, we gladden
the heart of the Father. Those of us who have kids
know what I mean when I say there was never a time
I withheld anything from my child when she had
just done something that made my heart soar with
gladness. And the end of this verse tells us that God
Himself wants to answer the transgression against us
because when someone offends one of His children,
it's the same as offending Him. God wants to bring
the answer. Don't you know His answer is going to
be so much better than any "punishment" we think
we're causing the other guy by our petulant attitude
of unforgiveness? Forgiveness is never for the other
guy. It's always for me. Forgiving another frees me,
not him. One of the best descriptions of unforgiveness

is this: "Unforgiveness is like taking poison and expecting someone else to die."

Just as unforgiveness is a form of bitterness, so is resentment.

Resentment says: "I will never forget what he did to me."

This spirit holds ill will in place and prevents us from healing relationships that have been damaged by offenses. It causes us to "hold a grudge." Resentment keeps a record of wrongs. God never does.

"If thou, LORD, shouldest mark iniquities, O Lord, who shall stand? But there is forgiveness with thee, that thou mayest be feared" (Psalm 130:3-4).

Maybe we've forgiven, or we think we've forgiven, or we've said, "I forgive you," but if it makes you feel sick to think about the person, there's still some bitterness in your heart that needs to be dealt with. So, while we may say, "I'll never forget!" God says:

"I, even I, am he that blotteth out thy transgressions for mine own sake, and will not remember thy sins" (Isaiah 43:25).

"For I will be merciful to their unrighteousness, and their sins and their iniquities will I remember no more" (Hebrews 8:12).

Another face of bitterness is retaliation.

Retaliation says:

"I'll forgive him when he's suffered enough."

"I want him to feel what I felt."

"I'll forgive him when I get even."
"It's time he paid for what he did to me."
To all these words of resentment, God says:

> Finally, be ye all of one mind, having
> compassion one of another, love as brethren,
> be pitiful, be courteous: Not rendering
> evil for evil, or railing for railing: but
> contrariwise blessing; knowing that ye are
> thereunto called, that ye should inherit a
> blessing.
>
> 1 Peter 3:8-9

But I say unto you which hear, Love your
enemies, do good to them which hate you,
Bless them that curse you, and pray for them
which despitefully use you. And unto him
that smiteth thee on the one cheek offer also
the other; and him that taketh away thy cloke
forbid not to take thy coat also. Give to every
man that asketh of thee; and of him that
taketh away thy goods ask them not again.
And as ye would that men should do to you,
do ye also to them likewise. For if ye love
them which love you, what thank have ye? for
sinners also love those that love them. And

if ye do good to them which do good to you,
what thank have ye? for sinners also do even
the same. And if ye lend to them of whom
ye hope to receive, what thank have ye? for
sinners also lend to sinners, to receive as
much again. But love ye your enemies, and
do good, and lend, hoping for nothing again;
and your reward shall be great, and ye shall
be the children of the Highest: for he is kind
unto the unthankful and to the evil.

Luke 6:27-35

And if something bad should happen to the person
who offended us, it is resentment and bitterness that
make us say, "Good! He deserved it." But God says:

*"Rejoice not when thine enemy falleth, and let not thine
heart be glad when he stumbleth"* (Proverbs 24:17).

*"Be ye therefore merciful, as your Father also is merciful.
Judge not, and ye shall not be judged: condemn not, and ye
shall not be condemned: forgive, and ye shall be forgiven"*
(Luke 6:36-37).

Bitterness carries us into anger, and sometimes
anger carries us into bitterness. Either way, it's a dead-
end street. Anger is an outward expression that cannot
be hidden. Words of anger are carried on a tone of
voice that is unmistakable and one with which we are
all familiar. Anger, which usually expresses itself in

accusation and self-accusation, begets hatred, hatred begets violence, and violence begets murder. Look at how murder is connected to bitterness: *"Wherefore is light given to him that is in misery, and life unto the bitter in soul; Which long for death, but it cometh not; and dig for it more than for hid treasures"* (Job 3:20-21).

Bitterness is such an insidiously evil spirit that those embroiled in its cauldron can reach a point of hopelessness where they long for death. It's a sort of "I'll show You, God!" attitude. "My life sucks, and it's all Your fault, God. Why don't You just kill me and get it over with? Put me out of my misery."

Another aspect of this connection between murder and bitterness is how we might feel when those we love are harmed or killed.

"Thus saith the Lord; A voice was heard in Ramah, lamentation, and bitter weeping; Rachel weeping for her children refused to be comforted for her children, because they were not" (Jeremiah 31:15).

It's a choice to be comforted, to receive emotional healing. We can make the choice to allow God to be God and heal our brokenness, or we can refuse His love and comfort. Holding on to bitterness causes pain and suffering to become entrenched in our hearts, hardening them and creating heart soil suitable only for growing wickedness.

"Thy way and thy doings have procured these things unto thee; this is thy wickedness, because it is bitter, because it reacheth unto thine heart" (Jeremiah 4:18).

When we agree with bitterness and allow it to rule our spirits, we are opening ourselves to a life of misery and loneliness. We also become vessels of dishonor in the house of the Lord because the bitterness that comes through our words defiles many. Most of the time, it doesn't even matter what we say; it's the spirit on which the words are carried that affects people. Bitter words drip poison that kills peace and pollutes purity.

"Looking diligently lest any man fail of the grace of God; lest any root of bitterness springing up trouble you, and thereby many be defiled" (Hebrews 12:15).

How do we "look diligently" to avoid failing of the grace of God? Love, love, love. Forgive, forgive, forgive. If we do not keep the commandment of love, some root of bitterness is sure to spring up, and defilement will begin. It begins with a troubling in our hearts and then spreads to those around us. Thank God for God! It is His peace and His grace that we can turn to, knowing He is a Master Gardener and can uproot anything in His garden (that's our hearts) that is displeasing to Him. The only responsibility we have is to allow Him access to dig out the wicked weeds and give Him free rein to reign! God, out of love for our souls, delivers us from the corruption of bitterness!

"Behold, for peace I had great bitterness: but thou hast in love to my soul delivered it from the pit of corruption: for thou hast cast all my sins behind thy back" (Isaiah 38:17).

It's time to tie this all back to envy and jealousy because we said bitterness is one of the spirits that promotes those evil sins in our lives. One of the best examples of this is found in the book of Acts. Let's look at this account and a few of the interesting insights the Lord has given through it.

> Then Philip went down to the city of
> Samaria, and preached Christ unto them.
> And the people with one accord gave heed
> unto those things which Philip spake,
> hearing and seeing the miracles which he
> did.
>
> Acts 8:5-6

The first insight is this: preaching should be accompanied by miracles. God said signs and wonders would follow His word. People listen when they do.

"For unclean spirits, crying with loud voice, came out of many that were possessed with them: and many taken with palsies, and that were lame, were healed. And there was great joy in that city" (Acts 8:7-8).

The second insight is that in the melee of signs and wonders, we have unclean spirits leaving people, and we see physical infirmities disappearing. This is an interesting insight because the number one block to physical healing has been shown to be unforgiveness. If there is bitterness, there is likely to be a compromised immune system. And please notice that people who are healed and set free create an atmosphere of great joy.

> But there was a certain man, called Simon, which beforetime in the same city used sorcery, and bewitched the people of Samaria, giving out that himself was some great one: To whom they all gave heed, from the least to the greatest, saying, This man is the great power of God. And to him they had regard, because that of long time he had bewitched them with sorceries.
>
> Acts 8:9-11

Okay, this fellow Simon had a reputation, and the people admired him.

> But when they believed Philip preaching the things concerning the kingdom of God, and the name of Jesus Christ, they were baptized,

both men and women. Then Simon himself
believed also: and when he was baptized,
he continued with Philip, and wondered,
beholding the miracles and signs which were
done.

Acts 8:12-13

Here we see Simon becoming a follower of truth.
He is now a believer, born again.

Now when the apostles which were at
Jerusalem heard that Samaria had received
the word of God, they sent unto them Peter
and John: Who, when they were come down,
prayed for them, that they might receive the
Holy Ghost: (For as yet he was fallen upon
none of them: only they were baptized in the
name of the Lord Jesus.) Then laid they their
hands on them, and they received the Holy
Ghost. And when Simon saw that through
laying on of the apostles' hands the Holy
Ghost was given, he offered them money,
Saying, Give me also this power, that on
whomsoever I lay hands, he may receive the
Holy Ghost.

Acts 8:14-19

Now, Simon sees a way to capitalize on this new God thing. He was successful as a diviner and sorcerer in the world. Now he wants to be successful in the kingdom, but he doesn't know how to go about it. He sees what others are doing, and he wants what they have. It is here that we see covetousness and envy creeping in. "They're doing that miracle thing. I want to do that miracle thing, so I'll buy it from them."

> But Peter said unto him, Thy money perish with thee, because thou hast thought that the gift of God may be purchased with money. Thou hast neither part nor lot in this matter: for thy heart is not right in the sight of God. Repent therefore of this thy wickedness, and pray God, if perhaps the thought of thine heart may be forgiven thee. For I perceive that thou art in the gall of bitterness, and in the bond of iniquity.
>
> Acts 8:20-23

Peter perceived—he knew, by the spirit of God within him, that Simon was jealous—and he called it "in the gall of bitterness." Simon repented, and so should we, maybe not because we were coveting another's ministry but certainly for thinking there is something we can do to obtain God's gifts or His

grace, other than simply believing in the Lord Jesus
and receiving His sacrifice on our behalf.

*"Then answered Simon, and said, Pray ye to the Lord
for me, that none of these things which ye have spoken come
upon me"* (Acts 8:24).

*Father God, I come before You in the mighty name and
authority of the Lord Jesus Christ, and I recognize there have
been times and circumstances in my life where I allowed
roots of bitterness to be planted in my heart. Lord, I ask You
to dig them up and burn them in Your consuming fire.*

*As an act of my will, I choose to forgive my mother and
my father and all those who have ever brought offense
against me in any way: through their words, their actions,
and even through their attitudes. I forgive them, Lord, and I
release them into Your hand, that You may bring an answer
to the reproach against You. I bless them, Father, each and
every one, with Your love and truth in their hearts and with
prosperity in their lives, that they may prosper and be in
health even as their souls prosper. That they may come to
know You and the power of Your resurrection.*

*Thank You, Father, for the ability to love those who hate
me, to bless those who curse me, and to pray for those who
despitefully use me. I repent to You, Lord, for participating
with spirits of unforgiveness, resentment, and retaliation
against Your children. I now see that I am the one who was
harmed, Lord, and I reject the fear and deception these spirits
brought into my life. I ask Your forgiveness for all the times I*

refused to forgive others, thinking the offense was too great. I
ask Your forgiveness for all the times I did not forgive because
I judged the person undeserving of forgiveness. I break all
agreement with unforgiveness.

I ask You to forgive me, Father, for holding feelings of ill
will against others and for keeping a record of wrongs, and I
break agreement with resentment. I ask Your forgiveness for
all the times I wanted others to suffer for what they did, Lord,
and I break agreement with retaliation.

Father, I ask You to forgive me for the bitterness that I
have entertained against You and others for the things that
have happened in my life. I know that many of the situations
and circumstances, the words spoken over me and against
me, the physical and verbal abuses I suffered were not in
Your plan for me, Lord, and I am sorry I agreed with the
enemy to accuse You. No longer will I listen to the voice of
oppression, affliction, and sorrow, Father, that would bring
me low and cause bitterness to grow in the garden of my
heart. Show me, Lord, what You want to deal with. I give You
permission to weed the garden of my heart right now.

I ask that You hide me from the secret counsel of the
wicked and from the insurrection of the workers of iniquity.
Take me into the secret place of Your abiding presence,
through the blood of the Lamb, where I can feel Your
heartbeat in my heart, hear Your whisper of love in my ear,
feel Your arms of strength around me, and fall into Your sea
of peace, in the name of Jesus. Amen.

Identifying and Overcoming Pride

"For the sin of their mouth and the words of their lips let them even be taken in their pride: and for cursing and lying which they speak."

Psalm 59:12

Pride is a strongman in the grouping of demons that often work together to hold envy, jealousy, and covetousness in place in our lives. There is so much to say about pride that we could write whole books on the subject and not cover it fully. But we're not going to do that because we are primarily interested in its basic characteristics and recognizing the nature and spirit of pride by the words it uses. Of all anti-Christ spirits, pride is perhaps the biggest, ugliest, and most destructive because every spirit of "self" dwells with and has its root in either pride or fear, or both.

The basic nature of Satan himself is pride, fear, and deception. He is at once the most fearful and the most prideful of all creatures. It was his pride that brought the wrath of God upon him. The moment iniquity was found in his heart, those arrogant and prideful thoughts that made him exalt himself above God, Lucifer was stripped of his position and cast out of heaven. It was then that Lucifer's name was changed, and he became known as Satan, which means "enemy of good."

> Thy pomp is brought down to the grave, and the noise of thy viols: the worm is spread under thee, and the worms cover thee. How art thou fallen from heaven, O Lucifer, son of the morning! how art thou cut down to the ground, which didst weaken the nations!
>
> Isaiah 14:11-12

"And he said unto them, I beheld Satan as lightning fall from heaven" (Luke 10:18).

The cause of the destruction of Satan by God were the prideful words he spoke in his heart. Satan said five things, and all of them began the same way: "I will!" Pride is centered on self. It's all about me. In pride, we make ourselves gods over our lives, rather than turning our lives over to God. "I, me, my, and mine" become the principal guiding force to all our actions and our attitudes. Who knows better than me what's best for me?

Pride says: "No one knows better than me what's best for me."

And that includes God. He is one of the "no ones" who must take a back seat to the self-focus of pride. We're going to look at the things Satan said in his heart and how they relate to us, how we have the same attitudes and often don't even realize it.

> For thou hast said in thine heart, I will ascend into heaven, I will exalt my throne above the stars of God: I will sit also upon the mount of the congregation, in the sides of the north: I will ascend above the heights of the clouds; I will be like the most High.
>
> Isaiah 14:13-14

Satan said in his heart, "I will ascend." In pride, we say the same thing. I will climb up. I will climb up socially. I will climb up financially. I will climb up spiritually, whatever it is. Pride says, "I can do it myself." It doesn't matter what the "it" is, "I can do it myself" are words of pride. "I don't need your help. I can do it myself." "I don't need God, I can do it myself." Any time we get caught up in our personal talents or abilities to see us through a project, no matter what it is, we are in pride.

Pride says: "I can do it myself."

God says: *"I am the vine, ye are the branches: He that abideth in me, and I in him, the same bringeth forth much fruit: for without me ye can do nothing"* (John 15:5).

Even Jesus Christ Himself did not act independently when He walked this earth as a man. He admitted His dependence on the Father: "I can of mine own self do nothing: as I hear, I judge: and my judgment is just; because I seek not mine own will, but the will of the Father which hath sent me" (John 5:30).

What is "nothing"? "Nothing" in this verse means "not even one man, woman or thing."[6] Now, if Jesus could do nothing, not even one thing, on His own, who are we to think we can? It is pride that gives us the words "I can do it myself."

Satan said, "I will exalt my throne above the stars of God." We say, "I'm gonna be the best!" Pride tells us it's not good enough to simply do our best, we have to be the best at what we do. Numero uno. Number one. I have to be the first, greatest, fastest, prettiest, smartest, best at the thing, whatever the thing is. I'm on top, or will be. That is an aspect of pride that calls forth lots of nasty cousins to come and play in our lives—spirits of performance and perfection, spirits of rejection and self-rejection, spirits of competition and compromise.

Pride says: "I have to be the best!"

God says:

"But ye shall not be so: but he that is greatest among you, let him be as the younger; and he that is chief, as he that doth serve" (Luke 22:26).

"For whosoever exalteth himself shall be abased; and he that humbleth himself shall be exalted" (Luke 14:11).

Satan said, "I will sit upon the mount of the congregation in the sides of the north." We say, "I should have the place of favor in the assembly." We tend to think in our hearts that if we were in charge of things, it would be better for everyone involved. And, of course, at the same time, we would be in a position to be admired by others. That's what we want. Recognition. When we allow these kinds of thoughts to hang around, and we begin to pet them, we also think we deserve the place of favor, all the time, no matter what. This makes us miserable in the gifts and talents God has given us. It puts us in a place where we can't be happy when someone else is doing something we're capable of doing, especially since pride has us convinced we could do it better!

Pride says: "Look at me! Favor me! Pick me!" "I deserve the favored position."

God says:

And when thou prayest, thou shalt not be
as the hypocrites are: for they love to pray
standing in the synagogues and in the
corners of the streets, that they may be seen
of men. Verily I say unto you, They have their
reward.

Matthew 6:5

This form of pride is also a manifestation of self-idolatry. "I'm more important, more spiritual, more trained, more whatever." In other words, we set up an altar to self-worship when we believe we should be the ones in the place of favor over another. But we are clearly told in Scripture that God is the One who promotes. It's His decision, not mine, as to whom He puts in the place of favor. He knows His purposes; I don't, nor do I have to.

Daniel answered and said, Blessed be the
name of God for ever and ever: for wisdom
and might are his: And he changeth the
times and the seasons: he removeth kings,
and setteth up kings: he giveth wisdom unto
the wise, and knowledge to them that know
understanding.

Daniel 2:20-21

And, of course, there is danger in setting up altars of self-worship and idolatry.

> Therefore speak unto them, and say unto
> them, Thus saith the Lord GOD; Every man
> of the house of Israel that setteth up his idols
> in his heart, and putteth the stumblingblock
> of his iniquity before his face, and cometh
> to the prophet; I the LORD will answer him
> that cometh according to the multitude
> of his idols; That I may take the house of
> Israel in their own heart, because they are
> all estranged from me through their idols.
> Therefore say unto the house of Israel,
> Thus saith the Lord GOD; Repent, and turn
> yourselves from your idols; and turn away
> your faces from all your abominations. For
> every one of the house of Israel, or of the
> stranger that sojourneth in Israel, which
> separateth himself from me, and setteth
> up his idols in his heart, and putteth the
> stumblingblock of his iniquity before his
> face, and cometh to a prophet to enquire of
> him concerning me; I the LORD will answer
> him by myself: And I will set my face against
> that man, and will make him a sign and
> a proverb, and I will cut him off from the

midst of my people; and ye shall know that I
am the LORD.

Ezekiel 14:4-8

When we say, even in our hearts, that it isn't fair
for someone else to have been chosen over us, we
set ourselves up to be brought down. We've heard it
said this way: "You will either practice humility or
suffer humiliation." Don't go there. If you think you
deserve something that someone else has, perhaps a
position of power or recognition, financial prosperity,
or whatever, consider that you may be falling into the
deception of pride that holds envy in place and sets up
altars to self.

Another thing Satan said in his heart was this: "I
will ascend above the heights of the clouds." By saying
this, he was putting himself in a place of superior
spirituality over all others. This manifestation of pride
makes us consider ourselves too spiritually important
because of what we know or what we've experienced
to perform a menial but vital service to the body of
Christ. In other words, we are too good to serve others
in a practical way. For example, the prideful person
will say, "If you're sick, I will come and pray for you,
but don't ask me to change your bed linens or wash
your dishes."

Sometimes, I need a bowl of chicken soup and someone to pick up the house more than I need a prayer! Pride makes us blind to the practical needs of people. Because we put such high emphasis on spiritual things, we become too good to meet practical needs.

Pride says: "I'll take care of the spiritual stuff, let others do the rest. I'm too important for that."

God says:

> If a brother or sister be naked, and destitute of daily food, And one of you say unto them, Depart in peace, be ye warmed and filled; notwithstanding ye give them not those things which are needful to the body; what doth it profit? Even so faith, if it hath not works, is dead, being alone. Yea, a man may say, Thou hast faith, and I have works: shew me thy faith without thy works, and I will shew thee my faith by my works.
>
> James 2:15-18

Finally, Satan said in his heart, "I will be like the Most High." Of all deceptions of pride, this one is perhaps the most prevalent. We so often put ourselves in God's place, especially if we have been offended by someone. We sit on the throne, judging our brothers and sisters as if we are God. This manifestation of pride prevents us from healing broken relationships. We think, "I'm right, you're wrong. So, you can come to me; I don't have to come to you. I'll get it right with God, but I don't have to get it right with you." When I have decided what's right and who's right, that it's me and my cause, I begin to act as if I am God.

There is a fine line in judgment. Yes, we are to judge the fruit of a person's attitude and actions. "You will know them by their fruits." But we are never to judge the person as unworthy of God's love or attempt to right wrongs against us by taking matters into our own hands. Our job is not to defend ourselves. Nor is it our right to punish other people by shunning them or talking down about them to make them look bad. Here's where the "run to the throne and not the phone" test reveals our pride. If we run to the throne of God and allow Him to be God in the situation, He will have us respond in an entirely different manner than we thought to respond. On the other hand, if we run to the phone to tell our friends all about how badly we were treated, we've just kicked God off the throne and put ourselves there.

Pride says: "I'm right, you're wrong. I'm the one that was wronged, so you make it up to me!"

God says: *"Moreover if thy brother shall trespass against thee, go and tell him his fault between thee and him alone: if he shall hear thee, thou hast gained thy brother"* (Matthew 18:15).

We are not to involve other people in the situation. When we are wronged, we are to approach the one who offended us and make it right. Lots of times, people are not aware of what they've done, and those who are can be won over by our humility. Even when the offense is obviously intentional, an approach of humility can bring healing to us and release God to work with the other person. The Word goes on to say that if the brother refuses to hear you, then take a witness and try again. We take a witness so that the person is less likely to twist or pervert what we say or do. Finally, if that doesn't penetrate the situation, we bring the matter before the church. Then and only then do we make the matter public.

We need to realize that an act of humility on our part will truly release heaven on our behalf, and God will handle things. We know this to be true from experiences in our own lives. The one that is most memorable to me is from years ago when I was elected president of one of our city's local volunteer organizations. There were two guys who were happy with the status quo, they had been in power for a long time, and they opposed every idea I presented. In addition, they slandered me at every opportunity in any way they could and really worked to undermine me in anything I wanted to accomplish. It was not pretty. I contacted them both, at separate times, apologized for anything I might have done to offend them, and asked for their help in moving the club forward. I offered to buy them lunch, to meet with me personally to get their input, and I began to speak positively about them to others. I refused to respond to the things I was hearing about myself, "Did you know so and so said blah blah blah?" "Did you hear that so and so blah blah blah?" To make a long story short, and it was a long story because it took quite a long time for things to settle, one of the guys would not respond at all and ended up quitting the club. But nothing he ever said about me swayed anyone because my actions and my words were pure toward him. The other guy became one of my best friends. He and his wife and I spent a lot of time together in fellowship, and God allowed me to introduce them to the baptism of the Holy Spirit and other good stuff. Since that time, we've all gone our different ways, but they are still very precious to me. The only times I've seen the first guy, he's been cordial and not nasty. God is good!

There's another thing we want to reveal about pride. Remembering that pride is a primary aspect of the nature of Satan, that's where we see it first and greatest, we want to go diving into a deeper understanding of what we call "human nature," or "the flesh." To do this, we have to go back to the garden and the book of Genesis: *"And God saw every thing that he had made, and, behold, it was very good. And the evening and the morning were the sixth day"* (Genesis 1:31).

Everything that God created was not just good, but very good. This means Adam was very good. There was no pride in him, no fear in him, no sin in him. His core being was exactly the same as that of God Himself, and 1 John tells us, "God is love." So we can conclude that Adam was love. That's who he was. Adam was created to be an expression of God's love on the earth. He was a spirit, just like God, but he was created as a human being. He had a body; he had flesh. And he had a soul, his mind, will, emotions, and desires. Having a body and having a soul defines us as human beings. His flesh was very good; there was no sin in his flesh. His soul was very good; there was no sin in his soul. Adam's nature was not sinful. It was very good. We're going to repeat this because somebody needs to get it: Adam was a human being, and Adam was sinless. The original human nature is very good, and we need to realize that!

Then Satan came along, and Adam decided to agree with his wife instead of with God. Did Adam lose his core being, the very essence of who he was, his godly nature of love? No, he didn't. That's who he was created to be, and you can't separate yourself from yourself. Satan could not remove the love nature. But he could pervert it, and he did. When Satan entered mankind through Adam, he brought his nature of pride and fear, and he twisted the love nature of Adam and turned it inward rather than outward.

Man became self-centered rather than God-centered, and the basic human nature, which is love, was perverted into self-love. The love is still there, but the focus is skewed. The "I will" of self became more important to mankind than the "Thy will" of God. When we hear of the carnal nature or sins of the flesh, we need to realize those are the work of the devil and not Adam. It is the pride of Satan, and not you, that is carnal and fleshly. We call it human nature, but it isn't. It's demonic nature, and human beings are not demons. As long as we think the carnal nature is "who I am," it will be impossible for us to separate ourselves from it because, once again, you can't separate yourself from yourself.

We can gain a great deal of insight and understanding of "the flesh" and the "carnal mind" by making a simple substitution in wording as we study Scripture. And we can make giant strides against overcoming the carnal nature of Satan within us by simply realizing the choice is ours. We are not bound to adhere to the thoughts of carnality or cravings of the flesh. Your flesh doesn't think, anyway. It's not believable to think your flesh has a desire of its own, without some prompting from the mind. We have the choice as to whether to yield to the "I will" of self-love expressed through us or the "Thy will" of God's love expressed through us. One of the greatest examples is found in Romans 8.

We're going to use the King James version, and our substitutions are these: where the word is translated "flesh" or "carnal," we will use "I will," and where the word is translated "Spirit" with a capital "S," indicating deity, which means the Holy Spirit of the living God, we will use "Thy will." If you have your Bible, follow along with us, and if you're using a King James, it will be easier to follow. Let's read the first fourteen verses of Romans 8 using our substitutionary words. This will help give you a really clear understanding of the foremost voice of pride, which is "I will."

> There is therefore now no condemnation to
> them which are in Christ Jesus, who walk
> not after the [I will], but after the [Thy will].
> For the law of the [Thy will] of life in Christ
> Jesus hath made me free from the law of
> sin and death. For what the law could not
> do, in that it was weak through the [I will],
> God sending his own Son in the likeness of
> sinful [I will], and for sin, condemned sin

in the [I will]: That the righteousness of the
law might be fulfilled in us, who walk not
after the [I will], but after the [Thy will]. For
they that are after the [I will] do mind the
things of the [I will]; but they that are after
the [Thy will] the things of the [Thy will]. For
to be [I will] minded is death; but to be [Thy
will] minded is life and peace. Because the [I
will] mind is enmity against God: for it is not
subject to the law of God, neither indeed can
be. So then they that are in the [I will] cannot
please God. But ye are not in the [I will], but
in the [Thy will], if so be that the [Thy will] of
God dwell in you. Now if any man have not
the [Thy will] of Christ, he is none of his. And
if Christ be in you, the body is dead because
of sin; but the [Thy will] is life because of
righteousness. But if the [Thy will] of him
that raised up Jesus from the dead dwell in
you, he that raised up Christ from the dead
shall also quicken your mortal bodies by his
[Thy will] that dwelleth in you. Therefore,
brethren, we are debtors, not to the [I will],
to live after the [I will]. For if ye live after the
[I will], ye shall die: but if ye through the [Thy
will] do mortify the deeds of the body, ye

shall live. For as many as are led by the [Thy will] of God, they are the sons of God.

Romans 8:1-14

with my substitutions as stated above

Praise the Lord! The "I will" voice of pride, the nature of Satan himself, has been revealed. About the only way to stay completely out of pride is to make certain every "I will" out of our mouths is in perfect harmony and alignment with the "Thy will" of God. When Jesus was in the Garden of Gethsemane, in such agony over what He was about to endure that He was sweating blood, He gave us the answer to pride and fear. He died to Himself completely.

> Then saith he unto them, My soul is exceeding sorrowful, even unto death: tarry ye here, and watch with me. And he went a little further, and fell on his face, and prayed, saying, O my Father, if it be possible, let this cup pass from me: nevertheless not as I will, but as thou wilt.
>
> Matthew 26:38-39

Had Jesus not died to Himself in that garden, He might never have gone to the cross. These verses tell us He didn't want to go through it. It wasn't His fondest wish to be shamed, spit on, beaten, tortured, and killed by being nailed by His hands and feet on a cross so that the very weight of His body would crush the breath out of Him. He said, "If there's any other way to do this, Father, let me out of this deal." But Jesus knew the strategic plan of God and maintained His steadfast alignment with God's plan. Being in God's strategic plan and receiving the everlasting benefits of His blessing is ever and always so much better than making our own plan and asking God to bless us in it.

Jesus took the cup He was appointed to drink. We have a cup to drink also. The result is the same. We die. But our dying is not physical death; it is soulish death. The death is the same as Jesus experienced in the Garden of Gethsemane; it is a death to "I will."

> What shall I render unto the LORD for all his benefits toward me? I will take the cup of salvation, and call upon the name of the LORD. I will pay my vows unto the LORD now in the presence of all his people. Precious in the sight of the LORD is the death of his saints.
>
> Psalm 116:12-15

When we take the cup of salvation, we accept and receive what the Lord did on our behalf. But we have an equal part in the covenant, and that is to give up what we want for what He wants for us, that is, dying to self and thus destroying the "I will" of pride.

In our experience, there is only one way to overcome pride forever, and that is to die to self.

There are three elements in the formula to become an overcomer.

"And they overcame him by the blood of the Lamb, and by the word of their testimony; and they loved not their lives unto the death" (Revelation 12:11).

We often hear about the first two, that we overcome by the blood of the Lamb and by the word of our testimony. But we need to realize the third element must be included, and that is loving not your life "unto the death." When we reach a point where our physical lives, our thoughts, our wants, our needs, and our desires are no longer our focus, we have become an overcomer. It is only when we are no longer ruled by the "I will" of pride that we can be completely used by God to fulfill our purpose and become the vital part of His strategic plan, which which is His will. Make this declaration and begin to overcome pride:

Father God, I come before You in the mighty name and authority of the Lord Jesus Christ, and I recognize I have entertained the spirit of pride in my life. I repent to You,

Lord, for every time I failed to recognize my need for You and others and acted independently.

Right now, I take "I can do it myself" out of my vocabulary, for I know that without You, I can do nothing.

I repent, Lord, for performance-oriented behavior, for thinking I have to be the best, not just do my best. I ask You to forgive me, and I ask that the curse be broken.

Forgive me, Lord, for wanting the place of special favor and for envying others who have it. I know that You have a place for me and will promote me to my place of special favor at the perfect time.

I repent to You, Lord, for the times I've been so heavenly-minded that I'm no earthly good, for thinking I need a more important job than serving the practical needs of my brothers and sisters.

And forgive me, Lord, for sitting on Your throne and acting like I'm God. Help me embrace and demonstrate the attitude of humility in all situations, Father, and give me the courage to step out to heal broken relationships in my life.

Lord, I am sorry for putting my will above Your will and for allowing "self" to rule my life. I ask Your forgiveness, and I ask that the curse be broken in Jesus' name. Amen.

Identifying and Overcoming Fear

"For God hath not given us the spirit of fear; but of power, and of love, and of a sound mind."

2 Timothy 1:7

The last demonic spirit we talked about was pride, which is a basic component of the nature of Satan, and as such, can easily become a stronghold in our lives. Another primary aspect of Satan's nature is fear. What does fear say? How can we know the underlying spirit is fear when we don't think we're afraid? That sounds strange, but it is true that oftentimes we are affected by some form of fear, even though we seem to be doing just fine and are certainly not exhibiting what we would consider symptoms of fear. Fear is very deceptive, especially when it hides behind some other evil spirit.

Once again, we will be unable to explore or fully explain every nuance of fear simply because the subject is too vast. So we will be primarily interested in the basic characteristics of fear and recognizing the nature and spirit of fear by the words it uses. Like control, fear has many faces. Some of them are timidity, insecurity, dread, worry, anxiety, sudden fear, specific fears (such as spiders or snakes or needles or blood, fear of the dark, and so on), general fear, panic, and terror. These are the main faces of the spirit of fear.

We said before that Satan is at once the most fearful and the most prideful of all creatures. The first thing Adam said after Satan invaded him with his nature was, "I was afraid."

"And he said, I heard thy voice in the garden, and I was afraid, because I was naked; and I hid myself" (Genesis 3:10).

Adam had heard God's voice plenty of times, and never once did hearing the voice of God make him afraid. Because God had never punished the man for anything, Adam would have had no point of reference to be afraid of God. Nothing had ever hurt him. The fear Adam expressed was not his own, it belonged to Satan. Satan was the one who had reason to fear God. He had already experienced God's wrath and didn't want any more of it! The first thing we need to realize, in a deep and lasting way, is this: fear doesn't belong to you. It belongs to the devil. Fear is an aspect of Satan's nature rising up to manifest and make us more like him rather than more like God. Read this declaration out loud: "Fear doesn't belong to me. I am not the one who is afraid. It's not me."

You see, as long as I think I'm the one who is afraid, I can't separate myself from fear. That leaves me ineffective in faith because fear and faith cannot coexist. They are equal in the spirit realm in that they both project into the future, and they both demand to be fulfilled, but they are equal opposites and cannot operate together. If I am in fear, I am not in faith. If I am in faith, I am not afraid. Remembering that faith comes by hearing, we need to be hearing from the right source, the truth of God.

"But whoso hearkeneth unto me shall dwell safely, and shall be quiet from fear of evil" (Proverbs 1:33).

What a powerful word of truth! If we hearken to the voice of God, if we attentively listen to the Lord, we will have no fear of evil. Because Jesus Christ defeated fear, the only thing fear has as a weapon is its voice. The best acronym for fear is false evidence appearing real. Anything that opposes the word and truth of God is a lie. An illness or symptom in our bodies is a lying vanity, and it is evil. It is false evidence that appears real and exists to render our faith ineffective. Does this mean we should ignore symptoms? Yes and no. First, we go to the Lord and get His counsel on the matter of our health issues. Then we do what He says we should do. God might tell us to go to the doctor for a diagnosis. He might tell us to pray. He might tell us to go to the intercessors in this ministry, or in your church, or have other believers lay hands on you and pray the prayer of faith. God could direct us in any number of actions. It could even be something really weird like, "Go dip in the Jordan seven times."

You can be sure, God's counsel will never be to worry over a symptom or illness. It will never be to focus on it and pet it or otherwise give it license to remain in you. God's counsel will never be to give up hope or faith by agreeing with fear. Symptoms are very often a deceptive device used by the enemy to distract us and pull our focus onto ourselves and off of the things of God. The devil wants us living in the spirit of the world and not the truth of the kingdom; he wants us caught up in the world system of facts rather than the kingdom system of truth. He wants us to agree that the false evidence that appears real is true so that he can bring it to pass in our lives.

Here's an example. One recent medical study concluded that a person with symptoms of a heart attack may not actually have the heart attack until the moment the following words are spoken or believed by the person: "I think I'm having a heart attack!" or the person imagines himself having a heart attack, getting a picture in his mind's eye. This may be why most emergency medical personnel, and many doctors, will not use the terminology "heart attack" anymore. They say something less fearful, like "cardiovascular insult" or something similar. The blood enzyme that proves a heart attack does not appear until after the patient has decided (agreed) that is the problem. Isn't that interesting! I believe this scenario is true for other diseases as well. We can fear a disease, think we might have it, convince ourselves we do have it, speak it out, and then contract it. The power of our words is equal in the spirit, whether we are speaking in fear or in faith.

"I believed, therefore have I spoken: I was greatly afflicted" (Psalm 116:10).

That is the progression, and many times that is how fear that is false but appears real actually becomes real in our lives. We believe. We speak. We are afflicted.

Voices of Fear. Section One

That being said, let's begin to look at the different faces of fear, their characteristics and language, and what God has to say about it. The first is timidity. This is actually the translation of the word "fear" in our opening scripture: God has not given us a spirit of fear, or timidity. It comes from a root word that means "dread" or "timid," and the spiritual application and implication is "faithless." Timidity is a form of fear of man. It makes us shrink from a task because we fear we might fail, or we fear we don't have what it takes to see it through, or we fear being recognized or noticed. It keeps us separated from people and social interaction because we fear rejection, or we fear people won't think we're worthy of conversation, or we fear we won't be able to think of something to say to them. Timidity is insidious. We say the timid person is just shy or introverted. No, he is afraid. Timidity is a manifestation of fear.

Fear in the form of timidity says: "I can't."

God says: *"I can do all things through Christ which strengtheneth me"* (Philippians 4:13).

Timidity says: "I'm not good at that."

God says:

> I thank my God always on your behalf, for the grace of God which is given you by Jesus Christ; That in every thing ye are enriched by him, in all utterance, and in all knowledge; Even as the testimony of Christ was confirmed in you: So that ye come behind in no gift; waiting for the coming of our Lord Jesus Christ: Who shall also confirm you

unto the end, that ye may be blameless in the
day of our Lord Jesus Christ.

1 Corinthians 1:4-8

*"Neglect not the gift that is in thee, which was given
thee by prophecy, with the laying on of the hands of the
presbytery"* (1 Timothy 4:14).

*Timidity says: "I won't know what to say. I don't know
what to do."*

God says:

Now when they saw the boldness of
Peter and John, and perceived that they
were unlearned and ignorant men, they
marvelled; and they took knowledge of them,
that they had been with Jesus.

Acts 4:13

And when they bring you unto the
synagogues, and unto magistrates, and
powers, take ye no thought how or what
thing ye shall answer, or what ye shall say:
For the Holy Ghost shall teach you in the
same hour what ye ought to say.

Luke 12:11-12

Isn't it good to know that we don't have to perform? That it's not up to me? God has given us the ability in Him to accomplish His purposes in our lives. We have the gifts within us, and within the gift itself is the ability to succeed. Timidity has no place in our lives.

"The wicked flee when no man pursueth: but the righteous are bold as a lion" (Proverbs 28:1).

When you feel like running away, and there's nothing chasing you, think of this scripture. It tells us timidity is wicked. Do not allow it to manifest and keep you from your destiny in God.

The second form of fear is insecurity, which is closely connected to timidity in many ways. Insecurity will also keep us from fulfilling our purposes in God, and its root is distrust. Feelings of insecurity are rooted in doubt and unbelief toward God. This spirit will manifest itself in one or more of several ways.

One of the manifestations of insecurity is a fear of lack. This can be the fear of lack of love, lack of companionship, lack of material things, or lack of money (which is also considered fear of poverty, a poverty mentality, or spirit of poverty). Looking at the insecurity as a fear of lack of love or companionship, we see that a usual manifestation is a kind of "clinginess" that makes a person appear very needy. It can also manifest by a person remaining in an abusive relationship simply because the person would rather have any relationship at all than risk having no one in his or her life. It is a fear of being alone.

This kind of insecurity says: "Don't leave me. I can't make it without you."

God says you are never alone:

"Have not I commanded thee? Be strong and of a good courage; be not afraid, neither be thou dismayed: for the LORD thy God is with thee whithersoever thou goest" (Joshua 1:9).

> Whither shall I go from thy spirit? or whither
> shall I flee from thy presence? If I ascend
> up into heaven, thou art there: if I make my
> bed in hell, behold, thou art there. If I take
> the wings of the morning, and dwell in the
> uttermost parts of the sea; Even there shall
> thy hand lead me, and thy right hand shall
> hold me.
>
> Psalm 139:7-10

Insecurity that manifests as a fear of poverty or lack can cause us to hold on to all kinds of useless things, "just in case." It may cause us to hide food or to hoard money. Entertaining this kind of insecurity may result in our striving for more, more, more all the time and never being satisfied with what we have. It leads us into self-preservation. It says things like, "I can't throw this away, I might need it one day." "If I don't do this, it won't get done." "I have to take care of myself because no one else is going to." God looks at things differently, and when we learn to trust Him, we can too.

Insecurity says: *"I can't part with my stuff."*

God says:

> Then Jesus beholding him loved him, and said unto him, One thing thou lackest: go thy way, sell whatsoever thou hast, and give to the poor, and thou shalt have treasure in heaven: and come, take up the cross, and follow me.
>
> Mark 10:21

"And such trust have we through Christ to God-ward: Not that we are sufficient of ourselves to think any thing as of ourselves; but our sufficiency is of God" (2 Corinthians 3:4-5).

Insecurity says: *"If I don't do it, it won't get done."*

God says:

"Take my yoke upon you, and learn of me; for I am meek and lowly in heart: and ye shall find rest unto your souls.

For my yoke is easy, and my burden is light" (Matthew 11:29-30).

"But one thing is needful: and Mary hath chosen that good part, which shall not be taken away from her" (Luke 10:42).

Insecurity says: "I have to take care of myself."

God says: *"But my God shall supply all your need according to his riches in glory by Christ Jesus"* (Philippians 4:19).

Another face of fear is dread. We've all experienced this. We may dread going to work, dread seeing certain people, or dread some event that is inevitable. I know that for a long time, I battled a spirit of dread concerning my father. He lived with me for the last seventeen years of his life, and toward the end, I allowed the enemy to steal so much of the joy of having him with me because I dreaded finding him dead one day. It was a horrible feeling—not knowing if when I got up in the morning, I would find him dead in his bed or somewhere else in the house. It was truly tormenting, and I had to get some help to overcome that fear. Please understand that it's okay to seek help. Don't let fear prevent you from reaching out!

Dread, basically, is a fear of change or a fear of confrontation. We don't want things to be different. We enjoy the comfort of knowing how things are and that they will remain as they are. Also, we don't like confrontation. We don't want to see or have to interact with a person who is contentious or causes us to give up some aspect of our peace. An impending event or meeting that we expect to be unpleasant can open the door to dread. The voice of the enemy becomes loud and clear, and we begin to agree with him.

Dread says: "I don't want to face this."

God says: "Then I said unto you, Dread not, neither be afraid of them. The LORD your God which goeth before you, he shall fight for you, according to all that he did for you in Egypt before your eyes" (Deuteronomy 1:29-30).

Dread says: "I'm afraid of what might happen."

God says:

> Only the LORD give thee wisdom and understanding, and give thee charge concerning Israel, that thou mayest keep the law of the LORD thy God. Then shalt thou prosper, if thou takest heed to fulfil the statute and judgments which the LORD charged Moses with concerning Israel: be strong, and of good courage; dread not, not be dismayed.
>
> 1 Chronicles 22:12-13

The next aspect of fear to explore is worry. Worry is fretting about something over which we usually have no control or a situation we are unable to change quickly. We worry about our health and the health of the people we love, we worry about our children, and we worry about what other people are doing or saying about us. We worry about whether or not we'll accomplish a task, if we will be accepted into a group, how we'll do on a test, how a medical procedure will turn out, or a hundred other things. Then we worry about what we don't have, what we can't do, or how we'll ever manage to get more than we have. If there is anything good about worry, it's that its main voice names itself.

Worry says: "I'm worried about..."

God says: *"Be careful for nothing; but in every thing by prayer and supplication with thanksgiving let your requests be made known unto God"* (Philippians 4:6).

"Be careful for nothing" means don't be full of care, stop worrying! The devil wants to keep us full of care, busily focused on ourselves and the negative possibilities of the future, so that we are totally ineffective in the business of the kingdom and what God has for us. The Lord cannot work with what we don't have and what we can't do. He is only concerned with what we do have and what we can do. When we bring Him what we have, He increases our prosperity in it. When we bring Him what we can do, He increases our ability in it. God is a God of increase. Remember, when it comes to the good stuff, God adds and multiplies, Satan divides and subtracts. Worry is one of the tools the enemy uses to do this. We've heard it said that 90 percent of what we worry about never happens, and the other 10 percent takes care of itself. If you think about it, that is really true. Consider the thing you worried most about last year, last month, or even last week. Where is it now? Can you even recall what it was that so consumed your thoughts?

I remember getting a call from a woman a few years ago at the beginning of the year. She was convinced she was going to die. She was so worried about her health that she was going to the doctor about every other week. She had signed up for every medical workup and test on the planet and swore her heart was doing weird things. She just knew she was going to have a heart attack or something equally devastating. We prayed, and I didn't hear from her for a few months. Then one day in late April or May, she called me again, sure she was dying. She had agreed with the enemy and allowed symptoms to consume her time, energy, and focus. I said, "Didn't we have this conversation in January?" yes "Didn't you think then you were about to die?" yes "Are you still here?" yes "So what have you done to advance the kingdom of God in the past four months?"

We need to realize that the enemy cannot take our lives unless we decide to give them over to him. Our lives are in the hand of God, and you and I are not leaving here one minute before we have fulfilled our purpose in God.

Another major voice of worry says, "What if?" "What if" is the question of the enemy, never the question of God. When it comes to worrying, "what if" is designed to carry us into worry for tomorrow, which is the number one cause of high blood pressure. Another form of worry for tomorrow is being deadline-oriented so that you push yourself to accomplish more and more in a shorter and shorter time frame. We end up striving to meet the challenges of tomorrow today, often not even knowing what those challenges will entail. So, while worry tries to get us to focus on all contingencies of every possible scenario (if this happens, then I'll have to do that, and so forth), God wants us free of worry for tomorrow and focused on today.

Worry says: "What if?"

God says: "Take therefore no thought for the morrow: for the morrow shall take thought for the things of itself. Sufficient unto the day is the evil thereof" (Matthew 6:34).

We need to answer the "what if?" with, "So what?"

One of the main things people worry about is sickness, death, and dying. When we are so self-focused on our bodies and the condition of our health that it consumes our time and our conversation, we're in trouble. If we are constantly seeking something that will heal us and keep us alive longer, and the somethings we seek are not God, we end up trying all sorts of things that can open doors for other problems. Concentrating on our afflictions keeps us from overcoming the very things that afflict us!

Worry says: "I'm afraid I'm going to die."

God says: "And they overcame him by the blood of the Lamb, and by the word of their testimony; and they loved not their lives unto the death" (Revelation 12:11).

Worry says: "I don't know how I'll pay my rent. What will we eat? I need some new clothes!"

God says:

> Therefore take no thought, saying, What shall we eat? or, What shall we drink? Or, Wherewithal shall we be clothed? (For after all these things do the Gentiles seek:) for your heavenly Father knoweth that ye have need of all these things. But seek ye first the

kingdom of God, and his righteousness; and
all these things shall be added unto you.

Matthew 6:31-33

We have a heavenly Father who loves us and will
take care of our basic needs. He supplies all our needs.
There is nothing we have that He didn't give us. And
there is nothing we truly need that He will not give
us. God is our provider, and He is our provision, so
we need to quit worrying about "stuff" and begin to
believe God so that we can enjoy our lives.

Another manifestation of fear to examine is
anxiety. Anxiety is an underlying feeling that
something is wrong, but you just can't put your finger
on what it is. You're bothered in your spirit, but you
don't know why. Anxiety can cause us to become
reclusive. It is a divisive spirit that separates us from
others. Anxiety steals our peace. It makes us afraid to
leave the place where we feel comfortable. The words
of anxiety include things like, "I can't leave here. Go
ahead without me." "Leave me alone. I'm okay." "I'm
afraid there's something wrong." "I can't sleep. I don't
feel safe."

Anxiety makes us turn to another comforter
other than the Holy Spirit in order to feel "normal"
or safe. This can be food, alcohol, drugs (even legally
prescribed prescription drugs), or something else.

Some people who are really anxious find a release in running or physically stressing their bodies to exhaustion in exercise. These kinds of practices are unhealthy and designed by the enemy to break us down physically and weaken us so that we become even more anxious. Anxiety can open the door to depression and other unclean spirits also. Anxiety is a sister to worry, and it is at its peak when we are "worried sick."

Anxiety says: "Go without me. Leave me alone."

God says: *"But if we walk in the light, as he is in the light, we have fellowship one with another, and the blood of Jesus Christ his Son cleanseth us from all sin"* (1 John 1:7).

Anxiety says: "I'm afraid something is wrong."

God says:

> For the mountains shall depart, and the hills be removed; but my kindness shall not depart from thee, neither shall the covenant of my peace be removed, saith the LORD that hath mercy on thee. O thou afflicted, tossed with tempest, and not comforted, behold, I will lay thy stones with fair colours, and lay thy foundations with sapphires. And I will make thy windows of agates, and thy gates

of carbuncles, and all thy borders of pleasant
stones. And all thy children shall be taught of
the LORD; and great shall be the peace of thy
children.

Isaiah 54:10-13

Anxiety says: *"I can't sleep. I don't feel safe."*

God says:

And I will set up one shepherd over them,
and he shall feed them, even my servant
David; he shall feed them, and he shall be
their shepherd. And I the LORD will be their
God, and my servant David a prince among
them; I the LORD have spoken it. And I will
make with them a covenant of peace, and
will cause the evil beasts to cease out of
the land: and they shall dwell safely in the
wilderness, and sleep in the woods.

Ezekiel 34:23-25

*"I will both lay me down in peace, and sleep: for thou,
LORD, only makest me dwell in safety"* (Psalm 4:8).

There are more faces of fear, and we still need to
discover the language of other types of fear, including
sudden fear, some general and specific fears, panic,

and terror. For now, though, let's break agreement with the fears we've identified so far and tear down the words these spirits have spoken through us.

Make this declaration and begin to overcome fear:

Father God, I come before You in the mighty name of the Lord Jesus Christ, and I recognize I have worn many faces of fear over the years of my life. I repent to You, Lord, for agreeing with the enemy and allowing fear to have rule over any part of my family, my circumstances, or me. I break agreement with fear in the form of timidity, insecurity, dread, worry, and anxiety.

Father, forgive me for those times I spoke the word of the enemy and said, "I can't; I don't know what to do or say; I'm not good at this or that." I realize that in You, Lord, I can because You are my strength and my ability. I recognize that in You, I do know what to do and say because Your Holy Spirit guides my words and my actions. I know that You, Lord, give me exactly what I need to accomplish the tasks set before me and that You make me good at what You've given me to do when I do it unto You and not myself.

Forgive me, Father, for the times I agreed with insecurity and spoke its words, for thinking and fearing being alone when You are always with me, and for not trusting You to provide for me. Lord, I ask that You help me become more faithful and less faithless.

I ask You to forgive me, Father, for dreading change or confrontation, and I ask You for a holy boldness and courage to face the most difficult challenges with joy in You.

Forgive me for worry, Lord, and all the times I spoke in agreement with it, projecting fear into the future and giving it an opportunity to afflict me. I'm sorry, Father, for fretting and focusing on my health, my life, my family, and my problems, instead of maintaining my heart steadfast in You and knowing You will take care of things in the way that is best for me, if only I allow You to. Help me stop letting the devil put his "what if" questions into my thought patterns and keep me focused on "what now," Lord, always listening for Your right-now answer.

Forgive me for anxiety, Father, and for allowing this evil spirit to steal my peace and separate me from You and others.

Father, I forgive my ancestors for any time they opened the door for any of these evil spirits to attach themselves to me, and I release them from responsibility for any curse that has come down to me. I give those generational curses to the Lord Jesus Christ right now, and I loose myself from the spirits that have held them in place. I declare I will no longer participate with timidity, insecurity, dread, worry, or anxiety. In the name of Jesus, I utterly reject every face of fear I have named. Thank You, Father, that as I break agreement with these fears, You break through in my life in a new way, giving me new hope, a new vision, and new effectiveness to advance Your kingdom on the earth. Amen.

If you prayed this prayer, take a few minutes to praise the Lord for what He's done for you before moving on to the next section about fear. Hallelujah!

Voices of Fear. Section Two

We've just examined some of the faces of fear and some of the words each face of fear may use. We showed how fear is very deceptive, especially when it hides behind some other evil spirit or disguises itself as something else. If you were to ask people if they are afraid, they'd likely say no. And yet, many of them are anxious or worried. Many people are timid or insecure. And many people dread something in their lives. Now, we know that these are all forms of fear. Oftentimes, we may be affected by some form of fear even though we seem to be doing just fine. Let's not be fooled by the devil anymore!

The subject of fear is far too vast to specifically address every single fear out there. Science has identified over 4,000 fears and named them. "Phobia" seems to be the last name of a lot of different fears. Phobia has a large family that thinks it has squatter's rights in Christian lives. The good news about this is that every name that is named has to bow to the name of the Lord Jesus Christ and fear in all its forms was defeated at the cross of Calvary. We will evict that family! We will also learn a little about other faces of fear, including sudden fear, panic, terror, and a few general and specific fears.

A few basic truths to remember are these: According to Scripture, fear is not an emotion, it is a spirit.

Another important thing to remember is that fear does not belong to you and me. It belongs to Satan. It is a part of his core nature and not ours. Our core nature is love and humility. Satan's core nature is fear and pride. We know this because we were and are created in the image and likeness of God, and God is love.

"Beloved, let us love one another: for love is of God; and every one that loveth is born of God, and knoweth God. He that loveth not knoweth not God; for God is love" (1 John 4:7-8).

"But whoso hearkeneth unto me shall dwell safely, and shall be quiet from fear of evil" (Proverbs 1:33).

This scripture tells us that as we attentively listen to the Lord, we will have no fear of evil. Fear is false evidence that appears real and is there to render our faith ineffective. God's counsel is, "Fear not." He tells us exactly these words 331 times in His Word. He says to us thirty times, "Be not afraid," and the phraseology another 175 times is, "Not be afraid." If we are attentively listening, actually hearkening to the Word of the Lord, we will not be afraid, which covers fear in all its forms. We won't worry, we won't be anxious, we won't be timid, we won't be insecure, we won't dread, we won't have sudden fear, we won't be afraid of height or bugs or snakes or participate in any of those phobias, we won't panic, and we won't be terrified. Praise God fear is defeated and we can now learn how it speaks so that we can tune it out and tune God in.

Let's look at sudden fear. Sudden fear is that moment that causes us to gasp or scream or cry out in some way. It's called sudden fear because it comes on us suddenly and can be triggered by any number of things, from a near accident in the car to someone jumping out at us from behind a door.

Sudden fear speaks in a frantic tone of voice: "There's a spider on your arm!" "Look out!" "Boo!" Sudden fear is often the result of what people consider practical jokes or just kidding around. Many people like to scare each other and think it's great fun. Halloween is an annual event that centers itself around a celebration of death and expresses itself in episodes of sudden fear. And most people, even Christians, believe it's okay, and even fun, to scare children and each other. Who among us never sat around a campfire telling ghost stories and then nearly jumped out of our skins when someone touched us or we heard a noise in the woods? It's really a shame that so many Christians were trained to laugh about being scared. We may have said it was all in fun and no harm to anyone, but God says otherwise: *"As a mad man who casteth firebrands, arrows, and death, So is the man that deceiveth his neighbour, and saith, Am not I in sport?"* (Proverbs 26:18-19).

According to this scripture, opening the door to sudden fear by playing a joke on someone is no different than murdering him. We all need to realize that fear, and especially sudden fear, can be deadly. Fear in the form of worry for tomorrow takes a slow toll on a person's life, but with fear in the form of sudden fear, death can be just as sudden as the fear. It is not uncommon for a person to keel over from a heart attack after being frightened. Sudden fear sets up an adrenaline rush in the body, increases the blood pressure, quickens the heart rate, shuts down digestive and other systems in the body, and marshals white blood cells to the skin in the event of injury. Physiologically, a lot goes on when we enter sudden fear. Gasping or screaming is just a small part of our involuntary physical reactions.

I want to take a moment to explain our view of adrenaline moments. God designed our bodies in such a marvelous way we can never hope to understand all that goes on in us. He provided a way for us to be able to accomplish "superhuman" feats in times of trauma, things like lifting cars off people. That's the purpose of an adrenaline rush. It's called the "fight or flight" response of the body. In times of true need, we have what we need. But when these bodily responses are called on repeatedly by sudden fear when there is no true danger, it becomes a dangerous programming practice that can break us down physically and emotionally. We begin to look for things to be afraid of, and this kind of thinking causes heart failure.

"Men's hearts failing them for fear, and for looking after those things which are coming on the earth: for the powers of heaven shall be shaken" (Luke 21:26).

Sudden fear says: "Boo!" or "Watch Out!" or another utterance of danger.

God says: *"Be not afraid of sudden fear, neither of the desolation of the wicked, when it cometh"* (Proverbs 3:25).

Everyone likely has some repenting to do for causing sudden fear in others and for allowing it to take occasion in us to cause problems in our thought patterns or our physiology. No more sudden fear!

Now let's look at general and specific fears. We cannot hope to name them all. But if you have become a victim, you know it. One fear we want to address is fear of food, medicine, and the environment because so many people are affected by these fears. How does it happen that the devil can so deceive us into believing that what we eat, where we live, or a legally prescribed prescription drug that has been tried and proven effective in managing symptoms can hurt us?

Let's start with food. Food allergies. Most food allergies come about because of word curses, generational curses, or trauma, and not because God created your body differently from everybody else's. Somewhere along the line, Grandma or Aunt Lois died after she ate peanuts, and now you can't eat peanuts. Guess what! This is often a familiar spirit, not a physiological aberration.

The spirit can be firmly entrenched because your family has always warned you not to eat peanuts, someone has told you that eating peanuts can kill you, your doctor has confirmed the dangers of peanuts to you because of your particular sensitivity, perhaps you've even had an incident where eating peanuts has closed your throat or affected your breathing, and so now you fully agree that you are allergic to peanuts. Fear of eating peanuts now controls what you put into your mouth.

You can substitute whatever foods you believe make you ill: milk, sugar, wheat, strawberries, it doesn't matter, but the source of the problem is the same. It is demonic. The manifestation of fear-based food allergies can be very different, but the right of the spirit to stay remains in our agreement with it. If you are in fear of something, or in doubt, which is a form of fear, about a certain thing, then do not foolishly sit down to a plateful of the thing.

Fear of food says: "I can't eat...(whatever)."

God says:

"I know, and am persuaded by the Lord Jesus, that there is nothing unclean of itself: but to him that esteemeth any thing to be unclean, to him it is unclean" (Romans 14:14).

"For meat destroy not the work of God. All things indeed are pure; but it is evil for that man who eateth with offence" (Romans 14:20).

In other words, if we believe and maintain that we cannot eat a certain food, then we will not be able to eat that food!

The apostle Paul has a lot to say about food in Romans 14, and he concludes with a pointed observation: *"And he that doubteth is damned if he eat, because he eateth not of faith: for whatsoever is not of faith is sin"* (Romans 14:23).

Whatsoever is not of faith is sin. One of the most amazing things to see is the transformation of people who have limited their foods for years and years, and then in one week of intense ministry where they receive truth, they begin to eat everything in sight. As their faith is built and they recognize how the devil has robbed them, they begin to step out in faith and allow themselves to be healed of the programming of "forbidden foods."

We are not advocating foolishness, especially if you've had serious reactions to certain foods. But it may be time for everyone to seek God more diligently in this area of food allergies because God said everything He created is not just good but very good. He did not make any edible plant or animal off-limits to certain of His children. They are for our nourishment and enjoyment. Don't doubt God. Say no to the devil and yes to food freedom!

The same thing is true for environmental issues, particularly smells. Chemicals in perfumes, cleaning agents, and so forth cannot affect us when we know our bodies are created with everything within us to overcome any outside factors that want to intrude and steal our peace. Demons know our fears and play into them. They will give us thoughts that are easy to agree with because of previous experiences.

Environmental fear says things like: "I can't be around _____ (fill in the blank) because I'll get sick with _____ (fill in the blank)."

This fear says: "I can't go, I can't clean my house, I can't see my friends, I can't wear perfume, I can't wash my clothes." I can't, I can't, I can't.

We can see how this face of fear holds us captive in our own homes, not feeling safe even there. Again,

God made this earth and all that is in it. The raw materials of everything manufactured by man were first made by God. The goodness of God's creation is inherent in all things, whether natural or man-made. It all belongs to God and is based on His handiwork. He did not make deadly stuff. We can die from chemical reactions because we believe we will!

Please don't think I'm making light of anyone's problems. I know how serious MCSEI (multiple chemical sensitivity environmental illness) can be and how programmed we may become to it. There was a time in my own life when I couldn't walk into certain retail stores or down the soap and detergent isles of the grocery store without having some sort of physical reaction. I no longer have that limitation. The truth is that if smelling perfume or bleach could kill a person, we'd all be dead and gone. We are essentially physiologically alike, and if your neighbor or your daughter can wear strong perfume, so can you. Think of the preparation of the bride of the king in Hadassah's day. Hadassah was the Jewish girl who became Queen Esther.

> Now when every maid's turn was come
> to go in to king Ahasuerus, after that she
> had been twelve months, according to the
> manner of the women, (for so were the days

of their purifications accomplished, to wit,
six months with oil of myrrh, and six months
with sweet odours, and with other things for
the purifying of the women;).

Esther 2:12

The perfumes and oils in which these women
soaked for a full year were very strong. The whole
palace probably smelled like an incense shop, a candle-
making factory, or a bath and beauty supply store. And
yet we do not read, either in Scripture or in history,
where any of the young women who were oiled up
daily, nor anyone in the area who was so continually
exposed to the olfactory assault of all the sweet odors,
died from the exposure. It didn't kill Esther, it didn't
kill the king's chamberlain Hegai, whose job it was to
keep the women, and it can't kill you!

As for medicines, we all need to be active
participants in our health care. Many people do die
from properly prescribed prescription medicines;
however, we should recognize that fear is behind
the destructive reaction in most cases. Some cases
are simply a matter of a person not knowing drug
interactions and taking something that wrongly
interacts with another something, which can be
another prescription drug, a natural remedy, or
a common food. But don't be afraid of medicine.

Sometimes we may need an antibiotic to assist our immune systems in fighting off an infection or disease. And there may be a legitimate need for other meds as well. None of us, at least no one I know, is totally immune to the "often infirmities" of life. It's okay to get some help now and then.

"Drink no longer water, but use a little wine for thy stomach's sake and thine often infirmities" (1 Timothy 5:23).

Those of you who know me know that I am not a big fan of medications. However, I do not hesitate to take something when I need to. The key is to consult the Lord about it first, pray over the medication, reverse the curse of the "contraindications, contradictions, and side effects," and then allow the medication to work as it was designed to work by not expecting something bad to happen.

I personally believe the legal ground for adverse drug reactions is in the written documentation of the drug itself. Declaring and writing the "side effects" and "contraindications" of the drug gives the enemy a perfect stronghold from which to operate. This documentation is a decree that is used in the spirit realm to bring to pass the contradictions and side effects in those who are open to accepting them. Many people read about the drug and then begin to expect the side effects. "Oh, it says I could have diarrhea for weeks after taking this. I'd better stay close to a bathroom for a while." I had a flash of revelation on our "King's Table" teleconference line one morning that drug contraindications and contradictions are called that because they contradict the Word of God. They are false evidence appearing real, a written declaration of fear.

Because these are written down and have, therefore, become a decree, we need to go to a higher decree to overcome them. That decree is the truth of God's Word. Find a scripture or many scriptures that speak of God's heart on the matter, and make your own decree, nullifying the decree written by the drug companies or the diagnostic decree written by your doctor. Here are a few we can all use:

"Bless the LORD, O my soul, and forget not all his benefits: Who forgiveth all thine iniquities; who healeth all thy diseases" (Psalm 103:2-3).

Make it personal: I bless You, Lord, and I do not forget Your benefits to me. You forgive all my iniquities, and You heal all my diseases!

"Then they cry unto the LORD in their trouble, and he saveth them out of their distresses. He sent his word, and healed them, and delivered them from their destructions" (Psalm 107:19-20).

Make it personal: Lord, I cry to You in my trouble because You are the One who saves me out of my distress. You sent Your word and healed me, Lord, and

You deliver me from destruction. You are healing and delivering me right now!

"But unto you that fear my name shall the Sun of righteousness arise with healing in his wings; and ye shall go forth, and grow up as calves of the stall" (Malachi 4:2).

Make it personal: Lord, I know that because I honor You and revere Your name, Your righteousness rises up and heals me. I will go forth like a young calf, full of energy and playfulness and tethered to You always!

"And the people, when they knew it, followed him: and he received them, and spake unto them of the kingdom of God, and healed them that had need of healing" (Luke 9:11).

Make it personal: I follow You, Lord, and I know You receive me. Teach me more about kingdom living, Lord, and heal me, for I have need of healing.

Next, let's look briefly at panic and terror, which are very similar faces of fear. Panic is a spirit of fear that manifests in extreme anxiety. A person in panic can't think straight, the blood pressure is usually elevated, the heart races. Anxiety attacks are a manifestation of panic. Usually, this is a spirit guide that is triggered to operate because of a trauma, although it may be something a person has carried for all his life, a spirit assigned by the enemy at or before birth because of generational open doors. Panic is rooted in Greek mythology, originating with the god Pan, who was supposedly the god of shepherds and flocks and the wilderness of the mountains. He was the companion of nymphs, and as such, panic is often associated directly or indirectly with situations of a sexual nature. It doesn't have to be but often is. The Greek god Pan, which would cause panic attacks, was built like a satyr (depicted as a creature having a man's torso and the hindquarters, legs, and horns of a goat).

As a prefix, "pan" denotes something universal or all-encompassing. For example, in a pantheistic religion, adherents believe everything is god. The voice of panic may speak in different ways, but the commonality is that every voice of panic is irrational. Panic opens the door to paranoia. To defeat panic, we must fully trust the Lord. Ask the Holy Spirit the source of panic in your life. If it is generational, forgive and release your ancestors for their participation with panic and stand in the gap for them. Panic can be removed because our God is the only true God. There is no other god who can stand in the presence of the living God. He alone is God, and He will destroy panic from our lives.

"The enemy said, I will pursue, I will overtake, I will divide the spoil; my lust shall be satisfied upon them; I will draw my sword, my hand shall destroy them" (Exodus 15:9).

Panic says: "There's something after me. I'll be caught. I'll be robbed. I'll be killed."

These are all things that panic will say, in one way or another. But then the Lord steps in!

> Thou didst blow with thy wind, the sea covered them: they sank as lead in the mighty waters. Who is like unto thee, O LORD, among the gods? who is like thee, glorious in holiness, fearful in praises, doing wonders? Thou stretchedst out thy right hand, the earth swallowed them. Thou in thy mercy hast led forth the people which thou hast redeemed: thou hast guided them in thy strength unto thy holy habitation.
>
> Exodus 15:10-13

"There is none holy as the LORD: for there is none beside thee: neither is there any rock like our God" (1 Samuel 2:2).

> There is none like unto the God of Jeshurun, who rideth upon the heaven in thy help, and in his excellency on the sky. The eternal God is thy refuge, and underneath are the everlasting arms: and he shall thrust out the enemy from before thee; and shall say, Destroy them.
>
> Deuteronomy 33:26-27

The final voice of fear we want to examine is terror. Terror is very much like panic, except that terror usually has more of a reason than a root. Terror is what we feel when faced with a situation of evil over which we seem to have no control. Our minds anticipate the worst, and terror rises up. Terror will normally manifest in a scream unless we are physically hiding from someone. It can also be a whimpering sound that we don't recognize, even though it's coming out of us. Terror that is not associated or directly connected to a real-life situation likes to visit in the night hours. This spirit wants to throw us into full-blown fear to steal our sleep, our peace, and our health. It is also one of the few spirits that we can physically feel: hair may stand up on your arms or head, the temperature may feel cold, there could even be the feeling of a cold breath of air on your body. It is terrifying.

The good news is that the Holy Spirit within us will calm our bodies and our minds if only we allow Him to do so. The power of God within us can utterly destroy terror and its effects on us. The problem is that in the moment, it can be somewhat difficult to turn our thoughts to the power of God. That is, however, the antidote for terror: knowing that God can handle it. He is Jehovah-Jireh, which literally means "God will see to it." And Jehovah-Jireh dwells in me. The true fear comes in because we somehow think we have to handle things when in actuality, we need only to draw out the power of the living God within us.

The voice of terror screams, cries out, or whimpers. There can also be a physical sensation.

God says:

> And every spirit that confesseth not that
> Jesus Christ is come in the flesh is not of
> God: and this is that spirit of antichrist,
> whereof ye have heard that it should come;
> and even now already is it in the world.
> Ye are of God, little children, and have
> overcome them: because greater is he that is
> in you, than he that is in the world.
>
> 1 John 4:3-4

It's time to repent for entertaining fear in our lives, make another declaration of faith, and step out into more freedom.

Father God, I come before You in the mighty name of the Lord Jesus Christ, and I thank You that Your divine nature of love overcomes and casts out all fear. I recognize I have worn many faces of fear over the years of my life. I repent to You, Lord, for agreeing with the enemy and allowing fear to have rule over any part of my family, my circumstances, or me.

I break agreement with fear in the form of fear of food, fear of chemicals, fear of smells, or fear of any other specific thing (if the Holy Spirit shows you something, break agreement with it now).

I break all agreement with fear of medicine and doctors, Lord. I know that You have given mankind many marvelous insights into Your greatness and allowed us to develop things that can assist our bodies in healing. Lord, never let me depend on medicine or the ways of man first before You, keep me always in tune with Your voice, ever in consultation with You, the Great Physician, concerning what I am to do and what medicines I am to take. Help me, Lord, to rid myself completely from the need for outside help, but never to condemn myself for getting help with Your guidance when I am truly in need.

I also break all agreement with sudden fear, and I repent for all the times in my life when I have caused sudden fear to have occasion to afflict others or me. I am sorry, Lord, for scaring other people and thinking it was fun and for laughing at sudden fear in others. I ask Your forgiveness, and I ask that the curse be broken.

I break all agreement with panic and terror, Lord, and I declare that Your presence in me is all I need to overcome panic and terror. I renounce the Greek god Pan and all his associates.

Father God, I forgive my ancestors for any time they opened the door for any of these evil spirits to attach themselves to me, and I release them from responsibility for any curse that has come down to me. I take those curses now and give them to the Lord Jesus Christ.

I now loose myself from any evil spirits, spirit guides, or familiar spirits that have held curses in place in my life.

I break all traumas from experiences that have opened the door for fear in my life or in the lives of my children.

I declare I will no longer participate with fear of food, fear of chemicals or the environment, fear of smells, fear of medicine or doctors, or any other specific fear.

I declare I will no longer entertain sudden fear, panic, or terror.

In the name of Jesus, I utterly reject every face of fear I have named. Thank You, Father, that as I break agreement with these fears, You break through in my life in a new way, giving me new hope, a new vision, and new effectiveness to advance Your kingdom on the earth. You only, God, are my Rock and my Salvation. Amen.

Identifying and Overcoming Accusation

"And when he was accused of the chief priests and elders, he answered nothing."
Matthew 27:12

Now we're going to take a look at one of the spirits that is a prime peace-stealer, accusation. When I sat down to put this book together, I asked the Lord, as I always do, to put it together the way He wanted it. As I pondered the subject of accusation, the Holy Spirit gave me an awesome revelation. It was one of those things we know, but we don't really know, something that is obvious, but we never really thought about before, and it is this: the spirit of accusation has a mission, and its mission is to steal our identity. The mission of accusation is to make us doubt who we are, bring confusion into our minds, and put us on the defensive. There have been many times in my life when someone would say something to me or about me, and I'd wonder, "Is that true?" Accusation is designed to make us doubt who we are so that we will accept a false identity.

The identity accusation wants us to have is shame-based. Accusation is a very belittling spirit. When we're on the receiving end of accusation, we know this well. Accusation makes us feel small, insignificant, and victimized. It can promote helplessness or hopelessness. It can create anger and defensiveness. The enemy is very happy when we react to the spirit of accusation with any of those responses because he then has us in his territory.

There are three basic things to know about accusation and how it draws us off track from kingdom business. First, we all want to respond when we are accused. It seems to be a natural response for us to defend ourselves. Second, we can use truth as an excuse to accuse; and third, accusation is a form of judgment colored with self-righteousness. Let's take a look at these revelations concerning accusation.

First, let's say this: it's very difficult not to respond to the accusation, but that is the pattern the Lord Jesus gave us to follow. When we can keep silent in the face of accusation, it amazes those around us. There is a wonderment attached to silence that causes people to think. They ponder the accusations, and, like Pilate, they will often conclude our innocence.

"And Pilate asked him again, saying, Answerest thou nothing? behold how many things they witness against thee. But Jesus yet answered nothing; so that Pilate marvelled" (Mark 15:4-5).

> And Pilate, when he had called together the
> chief priests and the rulers and the people,
> Said unto them, Ye have brought this man
> unto me, as one that perverteth the people:
> and, behold, I, having examined him
> before you, have found no fault in this man
> touching those things whereof ye accuse
> him.
>
> Luke 23:13-14

The next thing we should all realize about accusation is that accusation can carry truth but still be an abomination to God. The words that Adam spoke after being questioned by God were true, but they came from an accusing spirit. He said, "It was that woman that You gave me." In one sentence, Adam accused both Eve and God. Rather than taking personal responsibility for his actions, he accused another of his own sin. Most of us are, or have been, guilty of this very thing. Accusing another in our own sin is one form of being a "shovel Christian" and is very common to this evil spirit. When we're on the hot seat, we pass it on to someone else.

> And he said, Who told thee that thou wast naked? Hast thou eaten of the tree, whereof I commanded thee that thou shouldest not eat? And the man said, The woman whom thou gavest to be with me, she gave me of the tree, and I did eat.
>
> Genesis 3:11-12

Third, accusation is a form of judgment colored with self-righteousness. We tend to think of ourselves as not only holy and righteous but also as right and rightly appointed to correct others. Because we have the ability to judge, we tend to believe that's our job, and so we end up as fair game for a spirit of accusation to take up residence and put words in our mouths. The thing to remember is that we were never meant to judge one another. We are only meant to judge evil spirits, not people. To know an action or an attitude is wrong is one thing. To accuse a person of a wrong action or attitude is quite another.

Judge not, that ye be not judged. For with
what judgment ye judge, ye shall be judged:
and with what measure ye mete, it shall be
measured to you again. And why beholdest
thou the mote that is in thy brother's eye,
but considerest not the beam that is in thine
own eye?

Matthew 7:1-3

*"Therefore thou art inexcusable, O man, whosoever thou
art that judgest: for wherein thou judgest another, thou
condemnest thyself; for thou that judgest doest the same
things"* (Romans 2:1).

Because accusation tears down rather than builds
up, it is a dissembler. Accusation uses words that are
designed to subvert and overthrow another, which
makes it a froward, or perverse, spirit. The tone of
accusation is usually one of contempt. God does not
want us to judge and accuse others. He wants us to
judge ourselves and have mercy on others. We are
to bring restoration in meekness, not accusation in
judgment.

*"Brethren, if a man be overtaken in a fault, ye which
are spiritual, restore such an one in the spirit of meekness;
considering thyself, lest thou also be tempted"* (Galatians
6:1).

If we follow these scriptures, we can stay out of the
trap of being used by an accusing spirit to tear down
God's people. How do we recognize if we are in the
snare of accusation?

*Two of the words accusation uses most frequently are
"always" and "never."*

When we find ourselves using these words,
we should examine what we are saying and the
motivation behind it. "You never take out the garbage,
wash the dog, put the kids to bed, or whatever." That's
an accusing spirit. "You always think you have all
the answers. You always have to be right, have the
last word, or tell me what's wrong with me." That's
an accusing spirit. As for using truth as a weapon in
accusation, there's only one thing to say: God doesn't
like it. Before we speak to correct someone, we must
look into our hearts at the motivation.

Most of us know when we're on the receiving end
of accusation. We feel ashamed, we feel defensive, and
we may even want to lash out in retaliation. If we yield
to the temptation to answer the accusation with one
or two of our own, "Well, if you hadn't done such and
such, I wouldn't have done so and so," we can easily
fall into a cycle of accusation that keeps us ineffective
in the kingdom and unable to fulfill our purposes in
God. Silence is golden. If at all possible, we should
ignore the accusations. Pray silently and ask the Lord

for guidance and wisdom in the situation. Ask for His divine intervention and His peace to rise up within you.

There are times when ignoring the accusation is impossible. When the spirit of accusation doesn't stop at our silence, there is only one answer. No matter what the accusation against us may be, the most effective words to use against accusation are these: "I'm sorry you feel that way." And when another accusation follows, "I'm sorry you feel that way." Answer in love, with these words, as many times as it takes to silence the spirit. Many people have used this advice and discovered that it works. What happens when we answer this way is that we have acknowledged the person without engaging the spirit of accusation. Anything else is the start of another argument. We are not meant to defend ourselves or the truth. That's God's job. When we know in our hearts that our God is just and He will right all wrongs, we no longer have to lose our peace when we are accused. We can stand steadfast in Him, knowing that we do not have to defend ourselves.

"My soul, wait thou only upon God; for my expectation is from him. He only is my rock and my salvation: he is my defence; I shall not be moved" (Psalm 62:5-6).

We started out by saying that accusation is an identity thief because it causes us to feel ashamed, doubt ourselves, and even doubt God. This sets up separation from the Father, from other people, and even from myself, the person I was created to be. If the enemy can get me to agree with him that I am who he says I am, and not who God says I am, then my effectiveness in the kingdom will be destroyed. None of us can move into God's strategic plan in our lives when we do not recognize who we really are. Accusation puts labels on us, either through the words of others or thoughts injected into our minds by the enemy because of experiences we've had, generational issues we carry, or simple ignorance of God's Word and how to apply it into our lives. The Lord does not want us ignorant of the promises and benefits of our covenant, of His devotion to us, or of His faithfulness.

God also wants us to be fully aware of His opinion of each and every one of us. He never belittles us or considers us unworthy. When we hear words of accusation that make us feel unworthy, we should immediately reject them. They are not from God. We're going to go over a few of the lies accusation may tell us and what God has to say in answer.

Accusation says: "You're a failure. If you look up 'loser' in the dictionary, it will have your picture by it."

God says:

Behold my servant, whom I uphold; mine
elect, in whom my soul delighteth; I have
put my spirit upon him: he shall bring forth
judgment to the Gentiles. He shall not cry,
nor lift up, nor cause his voice to be heard in
the street. A bruised reed shall he not break,
and the smoking flax shall he not quench: he
shall bring forth judgment unto truth. He
shall not fail nor be discouraged, till he have
set judgment in the earth: and the isles shall
wait for his law.

Isaiah 42:1-4

This prophecy in Isaiah about the Lord Jesus Christ
encompasses who we are in Him. We are the servant
in whom the Lord delights. We have His Holy Spirit
within us. We shall not fail. There is no cause for
discouragement. We now have within us the fullness
of the Godhead, which is the love of the Father, the
power of the Holy Spirit, and the sound mind of Jesus
Christ, the Word. We are not defined by the past,
even if it was only ten minutes ago. Let it go, and as
it leaves, allow the shame of failure to go with it. To
fail at something doesn't make you a failure. As we
learn to walk in the kingdom, there may be times we
stumble and fall. Satan wants to keep us down through

accusation in the thing we did or said that caused the fall. God wants to raise us up.

"*For a just man falleth seven times, and riseth up again: but the wicked shall fall into mischief*" (Proverbs 24:16).

Have we failed? Oh, yes, at many things, but God has our future in His hands, and He will bring us into our strategic purpose if we allow Him to. The enemy will continue to accuse us of our past sins as long as we will listen. But when we close our ears to demonic lies and turn again to the Word of God, becoming doers of the Word and not just hearers, we will know godly success, and we will not fail.

> Is not this the fast that I have chosen? to loose the bands of wickedness, to undo the heavy burdens, and to let the oppressed go free, and that ye break every yoke? Is it not to deal thy bread to the hungry, and that thou bring the poor that are cast out to thy house? when thou seest the naked, that thou cover him; and that thou hide not thyself from thine own flesh? Then shall thy light break forth as the morning, and thine health shall spring forth speedily: and thy righteousness shall go before thee; the glory of the LORD shall be thy rereward. Then shalt thou call, and the LORD shall answer; thou shalt cry,

and he shall say, Here I am. If thou take away from the midst of thee the yoke, the putting forth of the finger, and speaking vanity; And if thou draw out thy soul to the hungry, and satisfy the afflicted soul; then shall thy light rise in obscurity, and thy darkness be as the noonday: And the LORD shall guide thee continually, and satisfy thy soul in drought, and make fat thy bones: and thou shalt be like a watered garden, and like a spring of water, whose waters fail not.

Isaiah 58:6-11

Accusation says: "You'll never be good enough."

God says:

"I will praise thee; for I am fearfully and wonderfully made: marvellous are thy works; and that my soul knoweth right well" (Psalm 139:14).

"Thou hast also given me the shield of thy salvation: and thy right hand hath holden me up, and thy gentleness hath made me great" (Psalm 18:35).

"For we are his workmanship, created in Christ Jesus unto good works, which God hath before ordained that we should walk in them" (Ephesians 2:10).

That we are all created exactly as God intended is a testimony that we are not only "good enough," we are exactly right. God knew each one of us, He created us with gifts and talents and abilities for His plan and purposes, and He died for us so that we could be free of the lies of accusation that tell us we aren't good enough. The value that God put inside each one of us is the reason Jesus went to the cross to take our sin on Himself. His sacrifice on our behalf made the way for us to remove all sin issues and all the demonic influences causing them. Jesus looked through the junk, the sin, the labels we accepted as who we are, and He saw our value. That's why He died: to restore us to the value that He put within us before the world was formed. He had to take our sins in order to make a way for that revelation to begin its work in us. We don't have to strive and struggle to be "good enough." God already sees us as perfect. Why settle for "good enough?" Let's begin to see ourselves as God sees us and step into the value of our core being.

Accusation says: "Nobody wants you."

God says:

"For thou art an holy people unto the LORD thy God, and the LORD hath chosen thee to be a peculiar people unto himself, above all the nations that are upon the earth" (Deuteronomy 14:2).

For I am persuaded, that neither death,
nor life, nor angels, nor principalities, nor
powers, nor things present, nor things to
come, Nor height, nor depth, nor any other
creature, shall be able to separate us from
the love of God, which is in Christ Jesus our
Lord.

Romans 8:38-39

"I am my beloved's, and my beloved is mine: he feedeth among the lilies" (Song of Solomon 6:3).

"I am my beloved's, and his desire is toward me" (Song of Solomon 7:10).

"His left hand should be under my head, and his right hand should embrace me" (Song of Solomon 8:3).

The Lord is excited about being with us. He loves us. He wants a relationship with each of us. Every one of us is His special treasure, chosen by Him, tucked away in His heart, held in His arms, completely covered by His love.

Accusation says: "You always mess things up. You can never do anything right."

God says:

"Verily, verily, I say unto you, He that believeth on me, the works that I do shall he do also; and greater

works than these shall he do; because I go unto my
Father" (John 14:12).

> And you, that were sometime alienated and
> enemies in your mind by wicked works, yet
> now hath he reconciled In the body of his
> flesh through death, to present you holy and
> unblameable and unreproveable in his sight.
> Colossians 1:21-22

> Blessed is the man that walketh not in the
> counsel of the ungodly, nor standeth in the
> way of sinners, nor sitteth in the seat of the
> scornful. But his delight is in the law of the
> LORD; and in his law doth he meditate day
> and night. And he shall be like a tree planted
> by the rivers of water, that bringeth forth
> his fruit in his season; his leaf also shall
> not wither; and whatsoever he doeth shall
> prosper.
> Psalm 1:1-3

Accusation can also make us lose our identity to
an illness. Often, a diagnosis can be an accusation.
Certainly, any agreement with a diagnosis that
contradicts the Word of God is an accusation against

Him. This would include allergies or syndromes (either physical, emotional, or mental), any supposedly incurable or terminal disease, and all commonly expected illnesses. It would also include spiritual conditions such as bipolar disorder, multiple personality disorder, dissociative identity disorder, addictions, accident-proneness, hereditary illnesses, abominable character traits of our ancestors, and the like. These are lies from hell that bring accusations: against God, first, and us, second.

When we lay claim to these things as a part of "who we are," we buy into the lie of the devil. We may have a disease, but we are not a disease and do not have to live with it or die from it. We are not defined by illnesses, syndromes, character traits of ancestors, inherited quirks, "bad blood," or any other unclean thing unless we agree to be defined in such a way. This is another kind of labeling designed to steal our identity.

Accusation says: "I'm sick. I have such and such disease."

God says:
"And the whole multitude sought to touch him: for there went virtue out of him, and healed them all" (Luke 6:19).
"Who his own self bare our sins in his own body on the tree, that we, being dead to sins, should live unto

righteousness: by whose stripes ye were healed" (1 Peter 2:24).

We've already been healed. The Word tells us so, and the Word is true. Here's what we have not yet grasped: truth is not subject to facts. The fact that we may be suffering from a disease of some kind or another is subject to the truth of God that we are healed of that something or other! Learning to speak the Word, bless our bodies, stand against the assignment of the enemy against God and us is a key to walking out of illness and into divine health. God created our bodies to heal themselves. We need to cooperate with that process.

Accusation says: "I will die from blah blah blah."

God says:

"For the law of the Spirit of life in Christ Jesus hath made me free from the law of sin and death" (Romans 8:2).

> Therefore doth my Father love me, because
> I lay down my life, that I might take it
> again. No man taketh it from me, but I lay
> it down of myself. I have power to lay it
> down, and I have power to take it again. This
> commandment have I received of my Father.
> John 10:17-18

Jesus laid down His life. It was not taken from Him. Consider this: Jesus was flesh and bone just like you and me. On the cross, He took on every disease known to man, and probably some we haven't even heard about yet, but not one of those things killed Him. He was born a man and operated on the earth as a man. Jesus had to agree with death for death to take Him. If we are indeed free from the law of sin and death, why do we agree to be bound by it?

Accusation says: "There's no cure for what I have. I just have to live with it."

God says: *"Beloved, I wish above all things that thou mayest prosper and be in health, even as thy soul prospereth"* (3 John 1:2).

The testimonies of people, just in this ministry, who have come out of the darkness and deception of something the world calls "incurable" are too many to number. We've said before, and we will continue to maintain it to be true, that God created our bodies to heal themselves of whatever goes wrong with them. From ADD/ADHD to mental and emotional breakdowns, to recurring curses of sinus or allergies, to bodies ravaged with cancer, we've witnessed the power of God to heal and restore. Our bodies should not rule us. How we feel should never dictate what we believe. We have power over our bodies; we just have to put the power of God into practice.

We are not the people that accusation has taught us we are. We are who God created us to be. Only the Lord Jesus has the authority to define our identity. No person, and no spirit working through a person, has that right. Let's break agreement with the labels we've accepted and strip those labels off our lives.

Father God, I come to You in the name and authority of the Lord Jesus Christ with thanksgiving and gratitude in my heart for who You are and who You have created me to be. I repent to You, Lord, for allowing spirits of accusation in myself and others to define me, and I declare that only the Lord Jesus Christ has the right to define my identity. Forgive me for accepting what others have said about me and for allowing their words to hinder my destiny in You. I am who You say I am, Lord. I am not a victim, I am a victor. I am not weak, I am strong in You. I am not sick, I am well in You. I am not a loser, I am a winner. I am not overcome, I am an overcomer. Forgive me, Lord, for defending myself, for becoming offended and defensive, for judging others, and especially for judging others in my own sin. Forgive me for keeping a record of wrongs against others and myself. I break agreement with the recording spirit and with the scrambler that would cause me to misunderstand others and be misunderstood by others. I break agreement with

all condemnation and self-condemnation, and I renounce a
false personality of accusation. Take me out of the miry pit
of accusation, Father, and put my feet on the solid ground of
Your love. You alone are my Rock and my Salvation. Lord, I
ask Your forgiveness for any time I have participated by my
words, my actions, or my attitudes with spirits of accusation.
Help me know Your truth, and be always motivated by Your
love. Father God, I forgive my ancestors for any time they
opened the door for accusing spirits to attach themselves to
me, and I release them from responsibility for any curse that
has come down to me. I take those curses now and give them
to the Lord Jesus Christ. I utterly reject accusation in every
form, and I ask to be free of all accusing spirits now. I submit
myself fully to You now, Lord, in Jesus' name, and ask that
You break all programming and patterns of accusation off
my life. Cleanse me of accusation and restore to me the joy of
Your salvation. Amen.

Identifying and Overcoming Confusion, Complacency, and Compromise

"For God is not the author of confusion, but of peace, as in all churches of the saints."

1 Corinthians 14:33

"And because iniquity shall abound, the love of many shall wax cold."

Matthew 24:12

"Why doth thine heart carry thee away? and what do thy eyes wink at, That thou turnest thy spirit against God, and lettest such words go out of thy mouth?"

Job 15:12-13

In this chapter, the Holy Spirit will reveal three spirits that, in the overall scheme of things, may seem insignificant but can cause tremendous damage to our lives and purpose in God. In order to live in the fullness of the blessing of the gospel of Jesus Christ, we must separate ourselves from demonic thoughts and words. If we are to accomplish that, we have to know of a certainty that the thoughts we have, the messages we get in our minds, are not always our own thoughts.

Anything which takes our focus off the living God and turns it elsewhere, usually to ourselves, our circumstances, our needs, and our desires, is rooted in darkness. Often, the shift is ever so slight, practically imperceptible. This makes the spirits working these "little iniquities" even more dangerous than what we consider to be the big guys. Seemingly small things, in the spirit, can be just as deadly to our destiny as the big stuff.

"Take us the foxes, the little foxes, that spoil the vines: for our vines have tender grapes" (Song of Solomon 2:15).

This verse tells us to seize and hold back the burrowers that would pervert and destroy the garden of God and prevent fruit from growing. (Remember, we are God's garden.) Some of those "little foxes," the burrowers that spoil the vines, are confusion, complacency, and compromise. These are three spirits that seem insignificant, as we said, but they pack a spiritual wallop that can knock us off course quickly and do so in such a way that we may not even notice, at least for a while.

It's wise to remember that it doesn't take a major shift to corrupt the journey. Even if we've been thrown only one degree off course, the farther we go, the farther from our destination we become. If your destination is Spain, you don't want to end up in South Africa. If your destination is to be conformed to the image and likeness of Jesus Christ, you don't want to end up looking like your Uncle Joe or Aunt Sally!

"For whom he did foreknow, he also did predestinate to be conformed to the image of his Son, that he might be the firstborn among many brethren" (Romans 8:29).

The Spirit of Confusion

One of the ways the enemy can keep us off balance, hoping to cause us to stumble and end up off course altogether, is through confusion. Confusion is that state of mind where nothing seems to come together, and we just can't think. It's as if our brains go out to lunch and forget to come back. On one side, our minds can be bombarded with so many thoughts and ideas, or opportunities and possibilities, or challenges and consequences, that it's hard to focus on what's important or even to identify the thing that is important. On the other side of the confusion coin is a sort of blankness of mind, where everything we were thinking or wanted to think about just disappears into an ethereal fog, and we wonder, "Where was I going with that thought? Did I even have a thought?"

Confusion works to cause us to doubt ourselves and to doubt God. It wants to render us incapable of making decisions, following through on plans, and developing projects. It will do its best to keep us focused on the endless possibilities of reaching a goal rather than the goal itself. "Let's go this way. No, wait, maybe that way is better. What about this over here? Have you seen this way? Here, go down this path, it looks good. Uh-oh, here's a fork in the road. Do I go back and start over? Should I turn right or left? Maybe I can just go this way for a while. Whoa! How about this?"

The Word makes it very clear that confusion is not something God sends our way: *"For God is not the author of confusion, but of peace, as in all churches of the saints"* (1 Corinthians 14:33).

Someone may be thinking, *Well, maybe it's not from God, but that doesn't mean it's a work of darkness. Maybe it's just me. My brain doesn't work like everybody else's.* Let's look at the Word to answer that: *"For where envying and strife is, there is confusion and every evil work"* (James 3:16).

This scripture lumps confusion into the same category as "every evil work." That would tell me it's not my brain that's the problem; it's my enemy that's the problem. This verse also tells us that envy and strife are open doors for confusion. So, if confusion is not of God but is instead a work of darkness, then we don't need it. Now that we know this, when confusion rears its ugly head, we can stop and say, "Wait a minute! I know where you came from, confusion, and God didn't send you. Lord, I repent for any envy or strife in my life, and I ask for Your peace that surpasses all understanding. Now, confusion, get out of my thinking! I have the mind of Christ, not a mind of confusion."

If there is anything good about confusion, it is this: we don't have to wonder if we're confused. Confusion is one of those spirits that name themselves.

Confusion says: "I'm confused."

God says: *"For who hath known the mind of the Lord, that he may instruct him? But we have the mind of Christ"* (1 Corinthians 2:16).

While "I'm confused" is the primary thing that confusion says, there are other common words used by this spirit. For example, "I just don't know..." This could be followed by another phrase. "I don't know what to say. I don't know what to do. I don't know where to go," and so forth.

Confusion says: "I don't know."

God says: *"But ye have an unction from the Holy One, and ye know all things. I have not written unto you because ye know not the truth, but because ye know it, and that no lie is of the truth"* (1 John 2:20-21).

We have an unction; what is an unction? The literal translation is "smearing." Our "knowing," the lack of confusion, comes from having contact with the Holy One, being smeared with His anointing of excellence and peace. When we are in contact with God, He furnishes us with what we need to make godly decisions so that we know what to do, what to say, and where to go. This confidence and clarity of mind doesn't come across as arrogance but humility because it is by His grace that we can maintain the peace necessary to dispel confusion and bring clarity into every situation. We know the truth, Jesus Christ, and the truth knows all things. The Holy Spirit within us witnesses to the truth, and the lies from hell, brought by confusion, have to go. Hallelujah!

Another big lie of confusion is this: "I can't hear God." One of the strategies of the enemy is to throw a barrage of thoughts into our minds so that it's difficult for us to tell which voice is which. Is that God? Is that me? Is that the devil? Who is that? When this happens, darkness whispers, "You see, you can't hear from God. God's not talking to you anymore." But He is. God never stops talking to us, but sometimes we stop listening and simply allow the barrage of thoughts in our heads to muddle the message of heaven. To think we don't hear God is a deception of darkness.

Confusion says: "I can't hear God's voice."

God says: *"My sheep hear my voice, and I know them, and they follow me"* (John 10:27).

We are the sheep of God, and we are designed to hear His voice. Even the unsaved hear God's voice. We know that to be true because if it were not true, no one would ever get saved! If the enemy could prevent us from hearing God's voice, he would, but he can't. The ability to hear God's voice is a part of who we are. It's how we are created. The enemy can't prevent us from hearing God's voice, but he can convince us God isn't talking to us, and he can throw in a bunch of mind fodder meant to cause us to listen to something other than God. This kind of strategy is like spiritual "white noise."

White noise is what we create in the natural to cover other sounds. If you don't want to hear the crickets chirping outside, you might turn on a fan to drown them out. That's white noise. When the devil wants to drown out the voice of God, he sends us spiritual white noise. God's still talking, but our ear is now tuned to something else. Another strategy the enemy uses to make us think we can't hear God is to make us think God's voice is our own. A lot of the time, people think they have a particular thought or idea because of fate or intuition, when in reality, it may be a prodding of the Holy Spirit. We might think, "Oh, that's just me." Confusion filters God's voice so that we're not sure who we're listening to, and when we think, "It's only me," we are likely to disregard the message.

Another major thing confusion says is, "My mind wanders, and I can't focus on what I'm supposed to be doing. I can't think." Here again, this is a lie from the enemy. Even when we say we can't think, we're thinking, just not on the right things. We have been created with marvelous minds. Consider Adam. He named every animal on the planet. There was no confusion causing him to throw up his hands in frustration and say, "I just can't think of any more names!" Our minds are creative; they are active; they are intelligent. We think! To say otherwise is to agree with hell. God wants our minds active with His Word and His plan and purposes, and He has given us what we need to succeed. Perhaps we need to retrain our brain to one of active meditation, which will keep us in contact with the Holy Spirit and allow His thoughts to permeate our being, bringing the wisdom of God into our circumstances.

Confusion says: "I can't think."

God says, "Think!"

> Finally, brethren, whatsoever things are true,
> whatsoever things are honest, whatsoever
> things are just, whatsoever things are pure,
> whatsoever things are lovely, whatsoever
> things are of good report; if there be any
> virtue, and if there be any praise, think on
> these things.
>
> Philippians 4:8

The Spirit of Complacency

A second spirit that seems harmless enough but is deadly is complacency. Complacency causes our hearts to grow cold.

"And because iniquity shall abound, the love of many shall wax cold" (Matthew 24:12).

This is the spirit that causes us to sit down and do nothing. It causes us to turn back when there is a breakthrough in moving ahead. The three primary things complacency says are, "I don't care," "It doesn't matter," and "I can't do anything about it." Complacency is very similar to a spirit of slumber in that we are lulled into a state of simply not caring what goes on around us. Not caring, that is, until the danger reaches our doorstep! Complacency is contagious, too.

When no one around us seems to care, we can easily fall into the same attitude.

Complacency can cause us to pass by a person who needs help because "it's not my problem." Like the priest and the Levite who avoided contact with the man who had been robbed, we can listen to complacency and go our merry way. Or when someone we know has something good happen to them, complacency is the spirit that gives us a "ho-hum, so what" attitude. I'm not involved, so I don't care.

Complacency says: "I don't care."

God says:

> For our comely parts have no need: but God hath tempered the body together, having given more abundant honour to that part which lacked: That there should be no schism in the body; but that the members should have the same care one for another. And whether one member suffer, all the members suffer with it; or one member be honoured, all the members rejoice with it.
>
> 1 Corinthians 12:24-26

Again, when Jesus told the parable of the good Samaritan, He was showing that we should extend a caring attitude outside the body of Christ. We are now to have compassion not only toward our brothers and sisters in Christ but also toward people we don't know.

> Which now of these three, thinkest thou,
> was neighbour unto him that fell among the
> thieves? And he said, He that shewed mercy
> on him. Then said Jesus unto him, Go, and
> do thou likewise.
>
> Luke 10:36-37

"I don't care" should never be a part of our vocabulary or our thinking as Christians. We are created to care. Don't let the little "I don't cares" work their way into bigger things. When we don't care about ourselves, we can't care about others. When we don't care about others, we can't care about God. When we don't care about God, we can't care about ourselves. This is a vicious cycle of complacency that will destroy our destiny if we allow it to continue to operate in our thoughts and lives.

"It doesn't matter" are also words used by a spirit of complacency. You and I both know that whatever the subject, this is a lie. It does matter. We only say it doesn't matter because the devil wants it not to matter. He wants us to be miserable creatures with no hopes or desires, and he has done a pretty good job of training us to disregard our hopes and dreams and lay aside our desires to succeed in advancing the kingdom. Let me tell you: as long as it doesn't matter to us, we'll go nowhere. My mother used to say, "If you aim at nothing, you're sure to hit it."

Complacency says: "It doesn't matter. It's none of my business."

God says: *"Arise; for this matter belongeth unto thee: we also will be with thee: be of good courage, and do it"* (Ezra 10:4).

This scripture is in reference to correcting behavior in the nation of Israel, but it can apply to many things. Basically, the Lord says it matters, whatever it is. The only place it doesn't matter is in respect of persons. It should make no difference to us whether a person has money, power, fame, good looks, or claims to be somebody. There should be no plumb line but Jesus Christ. This is what the apostle Paul meant when he said it didn't matter to him.

> But of these who seemed to be somewhat,
> (whatsoever they were, it maketh no matter
> to me: God accepteth no man's person:)
> for they who seemed to be somewhat in
> conference added nothing to me.
>
> Galatians 2:6

Complacency also says, "I can't do anything about it." Listening to this voice of the enemy results in our turning back from our purpose. If we don't see that we can make a difference, then we just won't do anything at all. Why is this? Because when we don't see a way to make it happen in the natural, we tend to forget the power we have in the spirit realm! We have been given access to every spiritual gift, which means we have the power of the cross, the resurrection power that raised Jesus from the dead. We can turn back and do nothing, or we can press in and do everything. Let's not be like the children of Ephraim:

"The children of Ephraim, being armed, and carrying bows, turned back in the day of battle" (Psalm 78:9).

Complacency says: "I can't do anything about it."

God says:

> Pardon, I beseech thee, the iniquity of this people according unto the greatness of thy mercy, and as thou hast forgiven this people, from Egypt even until now. And the LORD said, I have pardoned according to thy word.
>
> Numbers 14:19-20

Yes! We can do something about it, and this scripture tells us so. Our words have power, and our prayers can penetrate heaven and change circumstances and situations. We have the ability through God to pull down strongholds, cast out devils, heal the sick, and even raise the dead. Jesus gave us the commission to do something about it. Complacency wants to steal our destiny by making us believe we can't do anything.

The Spirit of Compromise

Now we're going to take a look at compromise. While complacency renders us unable to do anything, compromise causes us to do wrong things, often for right reasons. We all know we can do right things for wrong reasons. We can also do wrong things for right reasons. Compromise is a state of agreement in which nobody gets what he wants, but all the parties involved agree to settle for something "everyone can live with." The problem with compromise is that when we compromise the truth of God's Word, it can result in something we can die from, rather than something we can live with!

"Why doth thine heart carry thee away? and what do thy eyes wink at, That thou turnest thy spirit against God, and lettest such words go out of thy mouth?" (Job 15:12-13).

God considers the compromise of His covenant to be an abomination. Being a covenant child of God requires something of us, not just of Him. Why do we often think God has to be holy, but we don't? Some of the things compromise will say are, "God won't mind. He'll understand." "Maybe just this once." And "I'm doing this to keep the peace."

One thing we notice about all the great men of God in Scripture is that they did not compromise their faith. A great example of one who would not compromise is Daniel. Daniel had great favor with the king, which drew heavy opposition from others who wanted the same kind of favor. Daniel was elevated to a position of power, and there were those in lesser positions who wanted to bring him down. Compromise is one of the weapons used by envy and jealousy to pull us off course with God. Let's look at the plot against Daniel and his response.

> Then the presidents and princes sought to find occasion against Daniel concerning the kingdom; but they could find none occasion nor fault; forasmuch as he was faithful, neither was there any error or fault found in him. Then said these men, We shall not find any occasion against this Daniel, except we find it against him concerning the law of his God. Then these presidents and princes assembled together to the king, and said thus unto him, King Darius, live for ever. All the presidents of the kingdom, the governors, and the princes, the counsellors,

and the captains, have consulted together to
establish a royal statute, and to make a firm
decree, that whosoever shall ask a petition of
any God or man for thirty days, save of thee,
O king, he shall be cast into the den of lions.

Daniel 6:4-7

Here we have a group of people who are forcing a
situation in which Daniel must compromise his faith
and stop praying for a month or face death by being
devoured by hungry lions. Notice this: they weren't
trying to make Daniel renounce God or worship
another god; they just didn't want him worshipping
the true and living God. If we were faced with this
choice, don't worship for thirty days or die, how many
of us would have said, "Well, it's only for a month. God
won't mind. He'll understand." It seems to be such a
small thing, doesn't it? And it's reasonable to think
that God wouldn't want us to die when we could just
go along with the others, right?

Daniel would not and did not agree with that
kind of worldly thinking. The princes and governors
convinced the king to sign the decree, which could not
be changed, revoked, or rescinded, and the decree was
put in place. And what did Daniel do?

> Now when Daniel knew that the writing
> was signed, he went into his house; and his
> windows being open in his chamber toward
> Jerusalem, he kneeled upon his knees three
> times a day, and prayed, and gave thanks
> before his God, as he did aforetime.
>
> Daniel 6:10

As soon as he found out the decree had been signed, he went home and began to pray to our God. Of course, the conspirators were waiting for this to happen so they could catch and accuse him. Daniel was taken before the king and then thrown into the lion's den. Even though the king loved and respected Daniel and didn't want to do it, he had to live by the law he had signed. And we know the rest of the story.

> Then said Daniel unto the king, O king,
> live for ever. My God hath sent his angel,
> and hath shut the lions' mouths, that they
> have not hurt me: forasmuch as before him
> innocency was found in me; and also before
> thee, O king, have I done no hurt. Then
> was the king exceeding glad for him, and
> commanded that they should take Daniel up
> out of the den. So Daniel was taken up out of

the den, and no manner of hurt was found
upon him, because he believed in his God.

Daniel 6:21-23

If Daniel had compromised and gone along with
the decree, he would have no longer been innocent of
transgression. Likely, his enemies would have found
another way to attack. Because Daniel was steadfast
and did not waiver, not only was he protected, but also
his trial glorified God, and the king decreed Daniel's
God to be the living God whom everyone in all the land
must revere. Hallelujah!

I make a decree, That in every dominion of
my kingdom men tremble and fear before
the God of Daniel: for he is the living God,
and stedfast forever, and his kingdom
that which shall not be destroyed, and his
dominion shall be even unto the end.

Daniel 6:26

Compromise says: "God won't mind."

God says:

Take heed unto yourselves, lest ye forget
the covenant of the LORD your God, which

he made with you, and make you a graven
image, or the likeness of any thing, which
the LORD thy God hath forbidden thee. For
the LORD thy God is a consuming fire, even
a jealous God.

Deuteronomy 4:23-24

Compromise wants us to think that "just this once"
we can do something ungodly, and it will be okay.
The whole gang's going to the X-rated movie, and
you don't want to be left out. You don't want to be
ridiculed. You want to fit in. So you compromise, and
guess what! Now there is an open door in your life for
affliction. God doesn't punish us; He simply lets us
alone. Because we live in a cursed world, if we're in
it without God's presence, we're in trouble. The good
news is that when we repent, when we turn from
what we're doing and turn back to God, He is quick to
forgive us and restore us to righteousness. When we
commit wickedness, we step out of our rightful place
of rulership as kings.

Compromise says: "I'll do it just this once."

God says: *"It is an abomination to kings to commit
wickedness: for the throne is established by righteousness"*
(Proverbs 16:12).

Perhaps the most dangerous deception of compromise is that of "keeping the peace." We do things, or we fail to do things, so there will be no strife in the house. Perhaps we've been made to believe that if we go along with what others want to do, everything will be okay in our own lives. It's similar to feeding a monster hoping it will eat you last. Compromise to keep the peace usually only postpones the inevitable, and the end result is far worse than if we uphold our integrity with God instead.

Compromise says: "I have to keep the peace."

God says: *"When a man's ways please the LORD, he maketh even his enemies to be at peace with him"* (Proverbs 16:7).

Isn't it a much better idea to have God keep the peace than trying to do it ourselves? Let's purpose in our hearts to rid ourselves of confusion, complacency, and compromise, recognize these spirits when they come around, and refuse to comply with anything outside the covenant of God.

Father God, I come before You in the name of Jesus, and I humbly ask Your forgiveness for allowing confusion, complacency, and compromise to sneak into my life. Lord, I recognize that I have participated with every one of these spirits. I repent to You for listening to the lies of these works of darkness, for believing their lies, and for living their lies. Thank You for Your spirit of truth that dispels all confusion, complacency, and compromise from my life. I break all agreement with these evil things and will no longer speak their words. I pull down all words I have spoken that would bring these curses into my life or hold them in place. Right now, I declare:

> *I can think. I can hear You, God. I know all things because of Your Holy Spirit's unction.*
> *Right now, I declare:*
> *I do care. It does matter. I can do something about it.*

I have determined not to fall victim to the voice that tells me, "God won't mind," that I can compromise my integrity with God "just this once," or that I have to compromise to "keep the peace." You are my peacekeeper, Lord, and I believe Your word is true: when my ways please You, even my enemies will be at peace with me. Thank You for removing far from me spirits of confusion, complacency, and compromise. Amen.

Identifying and Overcoming Oppression, Affliction, and Sorrow

"Again, they are minished and brought low through oppression, affliction, and sorrow."
Psalm 107:39

There are three conditions somewhat common to mankind. Because of their commonality and the way they are intertwined with our emotions, we don't often think of these as being spiritually connected or as having demonic roots. The three conditions are oppression, affliction, and sorrow. These are the things that scripture says, "bring us low," and we all know that is true. What we may not realize is that these conditions are spiritual, not natural, and that they manifest in our lives because of spiritual forces that create physical circumstances. Yes, there are demons of oppression, affliction, and sorrow. Oppression and affliction are not just something caused by people and circumstances in the world, and sorrow is not just an emotion. By the end of this chapter, we will all have a better understanding of these conditions as evil spirits, know how they speak and what they say, and be able to banish them from our lives!

According to Scripture, whatever is not of faith is sin (Romans 14:23), so we can safely say that anything that takes our focus off the living God and turns it elsewhere—usually to ourselves, our circumstances, our needs, and our desires—is rooted in darkness. Oppression certainly can shift our focus off of God and onto ourselves.

The Spirit of Oppression

In the natural world, oppression is an unjust and often cruel exercise of power or authority. The oppression can come through a government edict or leader, a business policy or supervisor, or even a personal relationship. It brings a feeling of hopelessness and despair and causes people to feel weighed down in body or mind. The Bible calls this the spirit of heaviness.

Because oppression has a natural cause most of the time, we don't think of it as an evil spirit. By natural cause, we mean there is a real, natural-world reason we are oppressed, such as a cruel government or ruler. Pharaoh was oppressive to the Israelites, making slaves of them and requiring more of them than was physically possible in some cases. Unjust laws can create an atmosphere ripe for oppression to intrude. Ungodly domination of one person over another can cause oppression to manifest.

When we are subjected to these kinds of things as children, we may not recognize that oppression from childhood is often the root of depression in adulthood. These are real-life situations, and so we may easily believe that oppression is not a spirit but merely a resulting emotion, or "just the way it is." This kind of thinking will prevent us from fully separating ourselves from oppression and make us unable to live in the fullness of the blessing of the gospel of the Lord Jesus Christ.

When we are being oppressed, whether the oppression is real or imagined, we have a difficult time functioning normally. We are sluggish and unresponsive, or we may develop a sort of supersensitivity that causes us to "spark off" to those around us. Offense lurks at the surface of our emotions during times of oppression. This makes us quick to take offense and quick to give offense as well.

There is often an undercurrent of anger present in oppression. We resent our circumstances and all those we believe have caused them, but at the same time, we feel stuck and helpless to change things. If that sounds like you, aren't you glad you're reading this? There is a certain comfort in knowing there really is a reason for how we feel, and the reason is a spirit of oppression that was on the prowl and decided to take up residence with us! The people or circumstances that constrained us and seemed to be so overwhelming were simply vehicles used by the spirit of oppression.

"How God anointed Jesus of Nazareth with the Holy Ghost and with power: who went about doing good, and healing all that were oppressed of the devil; for God was with him" (Acts 10:38).

This verse tells us clearly that people are oppressed by the devil. Jesus went about healing all that were oppressed of the devil. It doesn't say Jesus went about healing all who were oppressed by their circumstances, their country, their bosses, their parents, husbands or wives, or any other person! Oppression is a weapon of the enemy. He may use a person to wield this weapon, but oppression is Satan's tool. So the first thing we need to do to rid ourselves of oppression forever is to recognize it for what it is, a weapon of the enemy and not an unfortunate byproduct of living in a cursed world. When oppression settles in on us, we need to remember the scripture in Isaiah, which tells us to put on the garment of praise for the spirit of heaviness.

> To appoint unto them that mourn in Zion, to give unto them beauty for ashes, the oil of joy for mourning, the garment of praise for the spirit of heaviness; that they might be called trees of righteousness, the planting of the LORD, that he might be glorified.
>
> Isaiah 61:3

This simple action of praising God will do more to lift oppression than any other. We have a good friend who gave an awesome testimony of what he had been through in his life. Through his testimony of what he went through and the way he handled it, I learned a very valuable life lesson. He said this, and I've used his words many times, "You can praise your way through anything." I found it to be true in my own life as I practiced what he said. His words became real to me. Praise your way through the difficult times, and you will overcome oppression, no matter what is going on around you.

Knowing that God is just and that He will right all wrongs is vital to being able to praise your way through trials and challenges with a pure heart. But we don't simply want to come out of oppression when it overtakes us; we want to avoid being overtaken! Oppression has a voice, and knowing some of its lies will help us avoid being oppressed in our circumstances. When we know the words oppression speaks, we can learn to turn away from believing the words of oppression and turn back toward believing the words of our living God. We're going to examine some of the things oppression says and God's answer to each.

Oppression says: "I'm stuck. There's no way out of this!"

God says:

> There hath no temptation taken you but such as is common to man: but God is faithful, who will not suffer you to be tempted above that ye are able; but will with the temptation also make a way to escape, that ye may be able to bear it.
>
> 1 Corinthians 10:13

We can all agree that oppression is negative, and the word temptation in the negative sense means "experience of evil" or "adversity." The Lord will not allow us to be stuck in a situation of being subjected to the oppression of others (whether individuals, governments, or companies). He makes a way out of it even when there seems to be no way out. We are not stuck! And here's some more good news. According to the prophet Isaiah, God even makes a way for us in the midst of our wilderness experiences, and He brings refreshing in our times of dryness:

"Behold, I will do a new thing; now it shall spring forth; shall ye not know it? I will even make a way in the wilderness, and rivers in the desert" (Isaiah 43:19).

We can use this scripture to lift us out of oppression, no matter how dismal the circumstances may seem.

Oppression says, "I don't feel like doing anything. I just can't seem to get motivated." This voice of oppression can be rooted in a spirit of heaviness, or it can come out of a spirit of slumber. When we feel lethargic, it's time to take a look at our faith. There could be a wavering of faith due to a religious spirit having closed off our understanding. This is where most of the Jews were and still are. They refused to believe the Messiah had come and was and is present, and so a spirit of slumber overtook them.

What then? Israel hath not obtained that which he seeketh for; but the election hath obtained it, and the rest were blinded (According as it is written, God hath given them the spirit of slumber, eyes that they should not see, and ears that they should not hear;) unto this day.

Romans 11:7-8

Those times when we refuse to believe Jesus has come and is present (because we are walking by sight and not by faith) may open us to the same spirit of slumber that causes lack of motivation and leaves us feeling oppressed.

Oppression says: "I don't feel like doing anything."

God says: *"For we are his workmanship, created in Christ Jesus unto good works, which God hath before ordained that we should walk in them"* (Ephesians 2:10).

When we don't feel like it and aren't motivated is the very time we should reach out and do something to advance the kingdom of God. The fight's not over when you make the decision, however. When you start to do something good, the devil will put this thought in your head, "Maybe God doesn't want me to do this. I don't really know what He wants, so I'll just wait until God shows me what to do." Here's a bit of advice:

When you don't know what to do, do what you know to do. In other words, if God hasn't given you a specific instruction, do what you know to be a good work anyway. Stop whining to God about your situation and begin to pray for someone else! Clean out your closet and take your old clothes to a clothing ministry. Mow your grass, and while you're at it, mow your neighbor's yard, too. Go over and clean your pastor's house. Take your friend some fresh-baked cookies. Look for a way to bless someone. It can be someone you know or someone you don't know, but be a blessing. Oppression will leave.

Oppression says, "There's no reason to try. It won't work." But God says, "Don't give up." Press in and press on. Endure the trials and tribulations and challenges before you because God is with you and will see that His purpose is fulfilled in and through you! That's good news, and even better news is that when we persevere, we are rewarded with the fullness of salvation.

Oppression says: "I give up."

God says: *"And ye shall be hated of all men for my name's sake: but he that endureth to the end shall be saved"* (Matthew 10:22).

That word "saved" is the Greek word sozo, and it encompasses full salvation, not just the aspect of being preserved in our spirits unto God so that we go to heaven. It means "healing," "preservation," "prosperity," "soundness," and "deliverance from evil." Praise God for the ability to persevere, keep on trying, be diligent, and not weary in the task set before us.

"Seest thou a man diligent in his business? he shall stand before kings; he shall not stand before mean men" (Proverbs 22:29).

The Spirit of Affliction

The second condition that brings us low is affliction. Affliction can be mental, emotional, or physical. Affliction is defined as severe distress that causes continued suffering or has a harmful effect. In the physical sense, and often in the mental and emotional sense also, the Bible calls this a spirit of infirmity. Affliction can be a spirit of torment as well. When it manifests as a disease in our bodies, affliction is easily identified as an infirmity; but when it manifests in our minds as schizophrenia or bipolar or some other form of insanity, we say it's only a chemical imbalance or some quirk of nature. In order to overcome affliction, we need to call it what it is, an evil spirit revealing itself. Let's stop trying to get along with it by saying affliction is something we have to live with!

Affliction is a spiritual condition brought on by a spirit that finds it simple to obtain our agreement with it most of the time. We begin to feel physically ill, and we say, "I think I'm coming down with something." Or we get a diagnosis from the doctor, believe it to be the truth, and immediately grab the phone to tell somebody, "I've got googamandu disease. Pray for me!" Then we tell everybody we know about "my" googamandu. It's as if we wear the thing as a badge. I can't tell you the number of people who claim a disease or infirmity or mental condition as their own, often without even realizing it. By doing this, they give the spirit behind the problem full permission to hold the problem in place. Affliction has everything to do with what we believe to be true.

"I believed, therefore have I spoken: I was greatly afflicted" (Psalm 116:10).

If we continue to lay claim to an affliction, no matter what kind it is, it is very unlikely that the affliction will go away. I personally don't believe we will be relieved of something we claim belongs to us:

"I can't wear that perfume because of 'my' chemical sensitivity."

"I'll probably not live to see my grandchildren grow up because of 'my' cancer."

"I'll have to take this medication for the rest of my life because of 'my' high blood pressure."

"Being in stressful situations triggers 'my' bipolar, and I might have an episode."

"I'm in constant pain because of 'my' neuropathy or 'my' sciatica or 'my' arthritis or 'my' fibromyalgia or 'my' whatever."

If any of those statements sounds similar to things you might be saying, stop laying claim to an affliction. It doesn't belong to you, it belongs to hell, and it isn't yours unless you claim it. You may have been diagnosed with a disease or condition, but that thing belongs to the enemy, not to you. If you have to talk about the condition at all, use new words: "I'm overcoming..." (whatever it is). Don't lie to yourself or other people by saying, "I don't have..." whatever it is, because, in the natural world, the diagnosis may be a fact. Take responsibility for the affliction because if you don't own a thing, you can't disown it. Then after you've taken responsibility for it, give the affliction to the Lord Jesus. It's a curse, and He's your curse-bearer! Thank Him, thank Him, thank Him that He took the thing on the cross with Him and you don't have to have it.

Facts of the world are what some people like to call "reality." We've all heard this or maybe said it ourselves: "I'm just being realistic. That's the way it is." Those are favorite words of the spirit of affliction. In truth, the spirit world is more real than the natural world, and the truth of God's Word is more real than the facts of the world. Facts do not always line up with the truth. God gives us a choice, and we get to decide which we will believe, and therefore, which we will experience. Do we want to believe the facts of the world, which bring a curse, or move to a higher place and believe the truth of God's Word, which brings a blessing? It's my choice.

"I call heaven and earth to record this day against you, that I have set before you life and death, blessing and cursing: therefore choose life, that both thou and thy seed may live" (Deuteronomy 30:19).

Affliction says: "That's the way it is. This is reality."

Shouldn't we do as God does and change the fact into truth, thereby living in a higher reality? God says:

> (As it is written, I have made thee a father of many nations,) before him whom he believed, even God, who quickeneth the dead, and calleth those things which be not as though they were.
>
> Romans 4:17

If we want to change our circumstances and banish the things that afflict us, we must change what we say about them! Change your words to change your life.

We should begin to prophesy over our bodies and call into being the health that is in our covenant. Call the things that be not as if they are, even though it seems foolish. This will overcome the world's reality and transcend us into heaven's reality.

> Where is the wise? where is the scribe? where is the disputer of this world? hath not God made foolish the wisdom of this world? For after that in the wisdom of God the world by wisdom knew not God, it pleased God by the foolishness of preaching to save them that believe.
>
> 1 Corinthians 1:20-21

Again, the Greek word for "save" is sozo, which includes every aspect of living an overcoming life, not simply being saved to go to heaven. It means "healing," "preservation," "prosperity," "soundness," and "deliverance from evil." All of it.

> But God hath chosen the foolish things of the world to confound the wise; and God hath chosen the weak things of the world to confound the things which are mighty; And base things of the world, and things which are despised, hath God chosen, yea,

and things which are not, to bring to nought things that are.

1 Corinthians 1:27-28

Even though these scriptures refer specifically to the institution of our new covenant with God (the changing of the guard, so to speak), they can apply to reversing affliction as well. We need to call forth the things that aren't yet revealed: our healing, our restoration, our prosperity, our soundness of mind, whatever. And in our calling forth the things that are not, our words will do away with the things that now are: the affliction in our bodies, our finances, our minds, or our relationships.

Affliction says many things. Not any of them are godly. In addition to saying, "This is reality," affliction also claims weakness and infirmity.

Affliction says: "I'm sick, I'm tired, I'm weak."

God says:

"Beat your plowshares into swords, and your pruninghooks into spears: let the weak say, I am strong" (Joel 3:10).

"He giveth power to the faint; and to them that have no might he increaseth strength" (Isaiah 40:29).

"But they that wait upon the LORD shall renew their strength; they shall mount up with wings as eagles; they

shall run, and not be weary; and they shall walk, and not faint" (Isaiah 40:31).

"Who his own self bare our sins in his own body on the tree, that we, being dead to sins, should live unto righteousness: by whose stripes ye were healed" (1 Peter 2:24).

The Spirit of Sorrow

The third condition we want to examine and rid ourselves of is sorrow. We should understand that not all sorrow is inappropriate, not all sorrow is ungodly, and sorrow is a legitimate emotion. God feels sorrow, and so should we. However, there is a kind of sorrow that leads to ungodly grief. Ungodly grief is a spirit of sorrow that brings us low and keeps us there. It makes us unable to function in the world. It takes us into a dry place where we can't get into the Word of God, and it can even cause us to accuse God.

We're going to look at sorrow from a couple of different perspectives. Sorrow is defined as sadness or anguish due to the loss of something precious to us. It's normal and godly to feel sorrow when a person close to us dies. The sorrow stems from the knowledge that we will not have the physical company of our loved one in this world any longer. We will miss the smiles, the conversations, the hugs, the presence of the one we love. It's okay to grieve that loss.

We can feel sorrow at the loss of physical objects that have sentimental value to us. Fires, floods, thefts, and other situations can leave us with memories that may now exist only in our minds, with no tangible objects left for us to touch or hold or look at for comfort or joy. It's okay to grieve those losses.

We can experience godly sorrow over the way we have grieved God by our behavior and sinful ways, both before we came into the saving grace of the Lord Jesus and afterward. That's a good thing. This is the kind of sorrow that will change our lives for the better.

> Now I rejoice, not that ye were made sorry, but that ye sorrowed to repentance: for ye were made sorry after a godly manner, that ye might receive damage by us in nothing. For godly sorrow worketh repentance to salvation not to be repented of: but the sorrow of the world worketh death. For behold this selfsame thing, that ye sorrowed after a godly sort, what carefulness it wrought in you, yea, what clearing of yourselves, yea, what indignation, yea, what fear, yea, what vehement desire, yea, what zeal, yea, what revenge! In all things ye have approved yourselves to be clear in this matter.
>
> 2 Corinthians 7:9-11

What's not okay is to dive into the pool of sorrow without the Holy Spirit. If you are a swimmer, you were likely taught as a child, "Never go in the water alone, always have a buddy with you. And never, ever, go into the deep end without a lifeguard on duty." Take that advice about sorrow because it can be a very deep pool with slick sides that make it hard to climb out. The Holy Spirit is our lifeguard in the pool of sorrow. If we choose to shut Him out, we can get into trouble quickly. The enemy creates a current designed to pull us under and hold us there long enough for a spirit of ungodly grief to attach itself to us and ruin our destiny.

We've known people who can't get past the sins of their past. They are drowning in sorrow and self-unforgiveness. Theirs is ungodly grief rooted in a warped sense of pride, in that they consider themselves so bad they are unworthy of forgiveness. We've known men and women of God who totally lost their way and their purpose in God when their spouse or one of their children died. They fell victim to ungodly grief connected to the loss and couldn't get out of it. Theirs is ungodly grief that is rooted in idolatry.

King David was pretty much in that state after the death of his son Absalom. He loved Absalom, even though this son conspired to take the kingdom from him. David was so wrapped up in Absalom that he almost lost the kingdom. Certainly, he caused distress among the nation. Though the Israelites had a great military victory, their king was so consumed in grief they couldn't even celebrate the conquest of their enemies.

> And it was told Joab, Behold, the king weepeth and mourneth for Absalom. And the victory that day was turned into mourning unto all the people: for the people heard say that day how the king was grieved for his son. And the people gat them by stealth that day into the city, as people being ashamed steal away when they flee in battle. But the king covered his face, and the king cried with a loud voice, O my son Absalom, O Absalom, my son, my son!
>
> 2 Samuel 19:1-4

You can read the entire account in 2 Samuel 19–20, and I think you'll find it very interesting. But basically, King David was putting his grief before his duty as a king to the people. He was essentially non-functional as the leader of Israel. The people were so disheartened and disgusted that there was an uprising, and a great threat loomed that the kingdom would be divided. This spirit of sorrow that settled on King David was rooted in idolatry. That is a source of ungodly grief. When we begin to worship a person, a place, or an object, and it is lost to us, the door is wide open for ungodly grief to set in and set itself up to destroy our lives and the lives of those around us, and even to change the course of history. Wow.

How do we judge whether or not we're drowning in that pool of sorrow? Here are a few clues:

- We can't read the Word.
- We find ourselves accusing God.
- We want to die.
- We find ourselves unable to function in our daily activities, and other similar, equally hindering manifestations may be evident.

Ungodly grief opens the door to spirits of accusation, condemnation, compromise, retaliation, resentment, anger, depression, suicide, and other stuff we don't want in our lives. Don't go there, and don't allow the enemy to take you there. How can you avoid ungodly grief? The easiest way is to know and trust God. If you don't know and trust God, then get to know Him, and you will find it easy to trust Him!

Knowing that God is the Just Judge who will right all wrongs can ease the sorrow of loss from theft and other circumstances where people seem to be the ones who caused the event that brought the sorrow. Knowing God gives us eternal vision, the ability to realize and be comforted that the separation from a loved one through death is a temporary condition and we have all eternity ahead of us, not just a few years on the earth. Knowing God makes us aware that we are never alone, that we are never rejected, unloved or unwanted, and that we have a Comforter with us at all times to lead and guide and direct us. Knowing God gives us assurance that we have purpose and destiny, that we are not dependent on loved ones, but on the One who loves us, that our lives are His and we can be prosperous and productive and joyful no matter what the condition of our lives may be in the eyes of the world. Knowing God eliminates self-pity and all the other self-spirits that cooperate with sorrow.

Ungodly sorrow says: "I can't be forgiven."

God says: *"If we confess our sins, he is faithful and just to forgive us our sins, and to cleanse us from all unrighteousness"* (1 John 1:9).

Ungodly sorrow says: "I want to kill myself."

God says:

For I am in a strait betwixt two, having a
desire to depart, and to be with Christ; which
is far better: Nevertheless to abide in the
flesh is more needful for you. And having
this confidence, I know that I shall abide and
continue with you all for your furtherance
and joy of faith; That your rejoicing may be
more abundant in Jesus Christ for me by my
coming to you again.

Philippians 1:23-26

Ungodly sorrow says: "I can't bear the pain of loss."

God says: *"Wherefore lift up the hands which hang
down, and the feeble knees; And make straight paths for your
feet, lest that which is lame be turned out of the way; but let it
rather be healed"* (Hebrews 12:12-13).

Ungodly sorrow says: "I can't go on."

God says:

Wherefore seeing we also are compassed
about with so great a cloud of witnesses, let
us lay aside every weight, and the sin which
doth so easily beset us, and let us run with
patience the race that is set before us.

Hebrews 12:1

It is by the grace of God that we can find joy in all situations and circumstances, and God's joy will overcome oppression, affliction, and sorrow.

> Then he said unto them, Go your way, eat the fat, and drink the sweet, and send portions unto them for whom nothing is prepared: for this day is holy unto our Lord: neither be ye sorry; for the joy of the LORD is your strength. So the Levites stilled all the people, saying, Hold your peace, for the day is holy; neither be ye grieved.
>
> Nehemiah 8:10-11

To the chief Musician, A Psalm of David.
The king shall joy in thy strength, O LORD; and in thy salvation how greatly shall he rejoice! Thou hast given him his heart's desire, and hast not withholden the request of his lips. Selah. For thou preventest him with the blessings of goodness: thou settest a crown of pure gold on his head. He asked life of thee, and thou gavest it him, even length of days for ever and ever. His glory is great in thy salvation: honour and majesty hast thou laid upon him. For thou hast made him most blessed for ever: thou hast made him exceeding glad with thy countenance. For

the king trusteth in the LORD, and through
the mercy of the most High he shall not be
moved.

Psalm 21:1-7

Pray this prayer and move out of oppression,
affliction, and sorrow:

*Father God, I make this psalm my prayer as a declaration
of Your greatness and in gratitude for Your goodness toward
me. You have made me a king, Lord, and I rejoice in Your
salvation and Your strength. Lord, You've put desires into
my heart, and You will bring them to fruition in my life.
You withhold nothing from me, Lord, and You go before me,
preparing my way with goodness and blessings. You give me
Your divine nature and authority. I asked for life, Lord, and
You gave it. You've even made me Your glory in the earth,
clothing me with honor and majesty. I am truly most blessed,
and as Your face shines on me, I am filled with gladness.
I trust You, Lord, and I know that I can be steadfast and
unshakable because of Your mercy. Thank You for Your Holy
Spirit presence, the resurrection power that raised Jesus from
the grave, dwelling in me.*

*Father, forgive me for participating so often and so deeply
with oppression, affliction, and sorrow and for allowing
those spirits to bring me low. I repent to You for denying the
presence of Christ in my life by my actions and attitudes and
opening the door for a spirit of slumber to make me lethargic.*

I break all agreement with oppression, affliction, and sorrow. I declare that from today I will put on the garment of praise for the spirit of heaviness. I will speak your truth over my mind and my body, dispelling forever the notion that affliction is a part of who You made me to be. I will be aware of pride and idolatry that would lead me into ungodly grief, and I will say no to them. As I submit myself under Your hand, Lord, I ask to be free of all these things. Restore to me the joy of Your salvation in every area of my life, Lord. I make my request to You in the name and authority of the Lord Jesus Christ. Amen.

VICKI SMITH BERDIT

Identifying and Overcoming Discouragement, Depression, and Despair

"For when they went up unto the valley of Eshcol, and saw the land, they discouraged the heart of the children of Israel, that they should not go into the land which the LORD had given them."

Numbers 32:9

"And I will set up shepherds over them which shall feed them: and they shall fear no more, nor be dismayed, neither shall they be lacking, saith the LORD."

Jeremiah 23:4

"We are troubled on every side, yet not distressed; we are perplexed, but not in despair."

2 Corinthians 4:8

No matter what time it is in our lives, this is a timely word because the three spirits we're going to talk about now are always ready to jump into our thoughts and cause us misery. We're talking about discouragement, depression, and despair. Like oppression, affliction, and sorrow, we can often think of these as simply being a part of living in a cursed world, that they are natural consequences of natural circumstances. But that is not the truth! Discouragement, depression, and despair are states of being that have demonic roots. There is an evil spirit that causes these three conditions, which we think are simply human emotions. As we've said, the majority of negative emotions are not negative emotions at all, they are evil spirits on assignment to mess up our lives!

Let's discover the way discouragement, depression, and despair speak. Knowing how these spirits operate, where they come from, and what words they use will allow us not only to overcome them but also to avoid them altogether. Won't it be nice to experience boldness and confidence rather than discouragement? To find happiness in our everyday lives instead of depression? To live in joy and not despair? That is our goal, so stick with it and discover that discouragement, depression, and despair are not a part of our identity, and we no longer have to entertain them!

Before we get into the definitions and origins of these three evil assignments from hell, we want to impart a very interesting insight into the prefix "dis." Most of your dictionaries, especially the newer ones, will tell you that "dis" is "to do the opposite of," "deprive of," "exclude," or "expel from." That is certainly correct. But if you are fortunate enough to have an older, unabridged dictionary, you will discover this definition of "Dis" with a capital D: "In Roman mythology, (a) the god of the lower world: identified with the Greek god Pluto; (b) his realm; the lower world; Hades."[7] In other words, Dis comes from hell itself, and words that begin with "dis" are more than simple opposites, they are rooted in the underworld!

All three of the things we're going to look at in this chapter have witchcraft as their foundation. Each one is a sting of witchcraft, but don't go into fear of evil. Most people think of witchcraft as the big stuff, such as voodoo hexes, Satanic ritual, Santeria, witches and warlocks, vampires, shapeshifters, and so forth. That's true, but witchcraft is simpler than that. Witchcraft is all about control. In its most simplistic definition, witchcraft is an attempt to control the actions or attitudes of another person or change the course of a person's life against his will.

The Spirit of Discouragement

When we discourage others from pursuing their course in God, we are actually participating in witchcraft. When we point out all the reasons why a person's vision or dream can't be accomplished, we are participating in witchcraft. Why? Because at the base of our words and actions is the desire to control that person. We say we don't want them to be disappointed, but in actuality, the reason more often is that we really don't want to see them succeed. Ouch.

Another reason we tend to agree with the devil and bring discouragement about another person's purpose is our own fear. We can see the danger and believe they don't see it. So we warn them, and we do it in such a way that they are discouraged and give up. We're happy and think we've done a good thing to "save" them when all along we may be thwarting or hindering the plan of God.

How many people have been called to do something in the kingdom or called to the nations, only to have family members or friends talk them out of the assignment or the trip because the place they're called is too dangerous or the task is too difficult? Discouragement is a sting of witchcraft that hinders us in our walk with the Lord. That's what happened in Numbers 32:9, our foundation scripture about discouragement.

The Israelites had a great promise, a sure promise, a God-given promise of a land to call their own. But the spies who were sent to scout the land came back with a fearful report.

"For when they went up unto the valley of Eshcol, and saw the land, they discouraged the heart of the children of Israel, that they should not go into the land which the LORD had given them" (Numbers 32:9).

The Israelites kicked the sure promise of God to the curb and believed the lie of the enemy instead. The result was that every one of them, with the exception of the two who stood for God's truth, died in the wilderness. None of the adults (except Joshua and Caleb) were allowed to see the fruition of the great promise of God. Discouragement can't destroy or remove God's promises, but it can remove us from them! The promise is real and true and will not change. But whether or not we realize it depends on us. We each have the choice as to whether or not to allow the sting of discouragement to stop our pursuit of what God has given us. We can press on to victory, or we can give in to discouragement. I hope everyone will be able to press on with more confidence and understanding after reading this book.

One situation, perhaps more than any other, can bring discouragement into our lives. This is when others do not value something that is of great value to us. This can be the same as murder to a dream, vision, or goal. And it is not limited to individuals but can pervade an entire nation and its purpose. One extreme example of this is found in 2 Kings, where we clearly see one of the stings of witchcraft. The method of witchcraft used in this account to discourage Israel was a blood sacrifice, and it had its intended effect.

> And when the king of Moab saw that the battle was too sore for him, he took with him seven hundred men that drew swords, to break through even unto the king of Edom: but they could not. Then he took his eldest son that should have reigned in his stead, and offered him for a burnt offering upon the wall. And there was great indignation against Israel: and they departed from him, and returned to their own land.
>
> 2 Kings 3:26-27

Even though the Israelites had the victory clearly in sight, after this human sacrifice, the armies of Israel turned back. The king of Moab killed his firstborn son. This was an act so repulsive and distressing to Israel that it completely discouraged them. To Israel, the life of the firstborn son was very, very precious. To see someone destroy in demonic sacrifice what they held so dear consumed them in discouragement, depression, and despair. They gave up when they were on the brink of victory. This was a deep sting of witchcraft that accomplished its purpose.

Notice that discouragement is most often worked through other people. But this does not mean we won't have times when discouragement can set in even though we are being encouraged by those around us. Hell likes to hammer us with our failures. When we try something, and it doesn't work, or it doesn't seem to work, there can be fertile ground for discouragement to begin to grow. Let's start with the words discouragement uses from within, in our thoughts, and then we'll look at some things discouragement may say through others' lips.

First, let's define discouragement. Discouragement is a lessening of courage or confidence through fear of consequences or being dissuaded by others. By the dictionary definition, discouragement is connected to fear. That makes sense. We become discouraged at something because we remember a past failure, and we are afraid we will fail once again. The truth is we never fail until we give up. If we don't give up, we haven't failed.

Discouragement says: "I might as well give up. I'll never be able to do this."

God says: *"Being confident of this very thing, that he which hath begun a good work in you will perform it until the day of Jesus Christ"* (Philippians 1:6).

If the Lord has appointed you to a task, He will see that it gets done. Don't listen to the voice of the enemy that says, "Give up!" God gave Daniel an excellent spirit, wisdom, and understanding to advise a king and govern a kingdom.

"I have even heard of thee, that the spirit of the gods is in thee, and that light and understanding and excellent wisdom is found in thee" (Daniel 5:14).

God gave Bezaleel, and others, skill in all manner of craftsmanship to oversee the construction of the sanctuary in the wilderness.

> Then wrought Bezaleel and Aholiab, and
> every wise hearted man, in whom the LORD
> put wisdom and understanding to know how
> to work all manner of work for the service of
> the sanctuary, according to all that the LORD
> had commanded.
>
> Exodus 36:1

God gave Solomon discernment to judge His people with great wisdom.

> Wisdom and knowledge is granted unto thee; and I will give thee riches, and wealth, and honour, such as none of the kings have had that have been before thee, neither shall there any after thee have the like.
>
> 2 Chronicles 1:12

God gave Moses a rod for confidence and a brother to be his mouthpiece.

> And he shall be thy spokesman unto the people: and he shall be, even he shall be to thee instead of a mouth, and thou shalt be to him instead of God. And thou shalt take this rod in thine hand, wherewith thou shalt do signs.
>
> Exodus 4:16-17

God gave Noah the blueprint for a big boat and the ability to build it: "Make thee an ark of gopher wood; rooms shalt thou make in the ark, and shalt pitch it within and without with pitch. And this is the fashion which thou shalt make it of" (Genesis 6:14-15).

God continues with the instructions: *"Thus did Noah; according to all that God commanded him, so did he"* (Genesis 6:22).

God gave David a slingshot and the skill to use it.

> And David put his hand in his bag, and took thence a stone, and slang it, and smote the Philistine in his forehead, that the stone sunk into his forehead; and he fell upon his face to the earth. So David prevailed over the Philistine with a sling and with a stone, and smote the Philistine, and slew him; but there was no sword in the hand of David.
>
> 1 Samuel 17:49-50

When we have so many examples of how God gives us exactly what we need in the way of tools and talents, how can we give up? The Lord is no respecter of persons. What He did for Moses and Daniel and Solomon and Noah and David and Bezaleel, He will do for you and me. Hallelujah! Stop listening to discouragement.

Discouragement that comes from others is still the voice of the enemy, and it's a voice that is meant to make us believe that "Everyone else is better than me, I'm not good enough." When we finally accomplish something we think is really good, someone moving in a spirit of discouragement comes along and says, "That's nothing, I do that all the time."

When this happens, we need to remember two things. It's pride that causes us to compare ourselves to others, and we are not here to please other people. God never meant for any of us to strive to be the best but only to do our best. And when we do our best, God is pleased, no matter how it turns out. It is our heart full of love for Him that counts.

Discouragement says: "That's not so great."

God says: *"And whatsoever ye do, do it heartily, as to the Lord, and not unto men; Knowing that of the Lord ye shall receive the reward of the inheritance: for ye serve the Lord Christ"* (Colossians 3:23-24).

One final word about discouragement: don't be the natural source of it! We all need to work at refusing to allow the enemy to use our tongues to bring forth his message of discouragement. Encourage others in what they are called to do. You and I don't know what God has in store for that person, how He might move, or what tools He has to give them. Rather than bringing a word of discouragement from hell, why not bring a word of encouragement from heaven?

"Heaviness in the heart of man maketh it stoop: but a good word maketh it glad" (Proverbs 12:25).

The Spirit of Depression

Depression is the feeling of dismay referred to in our foundation verse:

"And I will set up shepherds over them which shall feed them: and they shall fear no more, nor be dismayed, neither shall they be lacking, saith the LORD" (Jeremiah 23:4).

This verse also tells us the answer to depression, and that is to be teachable and receive the Word that is able to restore what was lost so that there is no lack. Depression is also one of the spirits in the progression of the stings of witchcraft. Depression is a lessening in activity or strength, sinking to a lower position, being sad or downcast. All of us have experienced feelings of depression at some point or another. Depression is a deepening of discouragement that makes it difficult to function at all. It makes us feel weak and tired and, like oppression, can bring on a spirit of slumber that sends us to bed. We sleep, not because we need the sleep but because it's a way to pass the time and escape the misery of being in our thoughts.

King David had lots of opportunities to be miserable and depressed, yet he found the way to avoid that condition. He gave us perhaps the best example of what we should do when the stings of witchcraft seem especially wicked and unfair. In 1 Samuel 30, we read the account of David and his army returning from war. The king was not out of the will of God; he was doing what a good king should be doing, leading his army. But while they were away, the Amalekites came up from the south and stole everything they had and burned their city.

David had done nothing wrong, and yet he lost his wives and children and possessions, and the entire city was destroyed. In addition to that, the men who had returned with him blamed him for their own losses, and they wanted to kill him! That would be more than enough to make a person depressed, to want to lie down and give up. But look what King David did. He responded to the ability of God, not the misery of the circumstance.

> And David was greatly distressed; for the people spake of stoning him, because the soul of all the people was grieved, every man for his sons and for his daughters: but David encouraged himself in the LORD his God.
>
> 1 Samuel 30:6

Because he sought the Lord and directed his thoughts to the Lord, King David was able to hear and receive the word of the Lord. The account tells us David pursued the enemy at the Lord's direction, overcame them, and recovered all.

Depression says: "I'm weak and miserable."

God says: *"Thou, O God, didst send a plentiful rain, whereby thou didst confirm thine inheritance, when it was weary"* (Psalm 68:9).

God refreshes us when things are bleak in our lives. Depression can't stand in His presence, the rain of His Spirit!

"Thy God hath commanded thy strength: strengthen, O God, that which thou hast wrought for us" (Psalm 68:28).

This is one of my very favorite verses and one I go to time and again. God commands our strength. He commands strength for us! That is powerful! We can know that the commandment of God will stand, especially at those times when we don't believe we can stand. His strength in us is all we need to overcome the sting of depression.

"Restore unto me the joy of thy salvation; and uphold me with thy free spirit" (Psalm 51:1).

The good news of the gospel: eternal salvation along with authority and power in this life and peace forever in the life to come is restorative, even in the worst of times. Knowing that God has put His spirit within me and I am totally free in Him is uplifting. That truth, and my belief in it, put depression on the run.

"And now shall mine head be lifted up above mine enemies round about me: therefore will I offer in his tabernacle sacrifices of joy; I will sing, yea, I will sing praises unto the LORD" (Psalm 27:6).

The joy of the Lord, which is my strength, pulls me out of depression and carries me above the "snake line," out of reach of the enemy. Do you know what the snake line is? Mountain climbers know that there is a place on the mountain where the atmosphere changes to such a degree that snakes cannot survive. When a climber reaches this point, he knows that he no longer has to worry about putting his hand into a crevice and finding a snake. He can continue his climb without fear. He is above the snake line. That's what God does for me when I focus on Him and the joy of His salvation, when I take my eyes off myself and the misery around me.

No more depression! We don't need pills and therapy to balance our chemical makeup or our thought processes. We need God.

The Spirit of Despair

Despair is an utter loss of hope. Hopelessness. Despair says, "It's no use. There's no hope." This is perhaps Satan's biggest lie. Hope is eternal, and it cannot be destroyed. We can lay it aside, it can be covered up with the weight of circumstances, we can forget we've got it, but it never really goes away. We were created with hope in our hearts. There is always hope. Hope is the thing that gives our faith substance. Without hope, faith has nothing to do. With hope, faith can work in and through love to accomplish all things. Despair wants us to think there is no hope in our lives, in our circumstances, in our relationships, in our finances, in anything.

Despair says: "There's no hope."

God says:

"We are troubled on every side, yet not distressed; we are perplexed, but not in despair" (2 Corinthians 4:8).

> Because thou shalt forget thy misery, and remember it as waters that pass away: And thine age shall be clearer than the noonday; thou shalt shine forth, thou shalt be as the morning. And thou shalt be secure, because there is hope; yea, thou shalt dig about thee, and thou shalt take thy rest in safety.
>
> Job 11:16-18

"But thou art he that took me out of the womb: thou didst make me hope when I was upon my mother's breasts" (Psalm 22:9).

One of the things despair does is this: It makes us think we've missed God, that we lost the chance to do what we were meant to do, told to do, or supposed to do.

Despair says: "It's over. I missed my chance."

God says: *"For there is hope of a tree, if it be cut down, that it will sprout again, and that the tender branch thereof will not cease"* (Job 14:7).

Despair also makes us think our lives are useless and we are without purpose.

Despair says: "I'm an accident. I wasn't meant to be born. I'll never amount to anything."

God says: *"Before I formed thee in the belly I knew thee; and before thou camest forth out of the womb I sanctified thee, and I ordained thee a prophet unto the nations"* (Jeremiah 1:5).

You know, every one of us has been ordained to something. It remains to be seen what that shall be! Even those of us who are quite sure we're where God wants us, doing what He wants us to do, we are also sure we won't remain in this place. There is always more with God if we're open to it.

> For thou hast possessed my reins: thou
> hast covered me in my mother's womb.

I will praise thee; for I am fearfully and
wonderfully made: marvellous are thy works;
and that my soul knoweth right well.
Psalm 139:13-14

Know that despair will be unable to stifle hope
without your permission. Hope is in our hearts
because the Lord Himself is our hope. Despair doesn't
stand a chance when we know the Lord!

The LORD also shall roar out of Zion, and
utter his voice from Jerusalem; and the
heavens and the earth shall shake: but the
LORD will be the hope of his people, and the
strength of the children of Israel.
Joel 3:16

Here are a few scriptures to ponder during those
times when despair comes knocking at the door and
you feel hopelessness creeping in:

This I recall to my mind, therefore have I
hope. It is of the LORD'S mercies that we are
not consumed, because his compassions fail
not. They are new every morning: great is thy
faithfulness. The LORD is my portion, saith
my soul; therefore will I hope in him. The

LORD is good unto them that wait for him,
to the soul that seeketh him. It is good that
a man should both hope and quietly wait for
the salvation of the LORD.

Lamentations 3:21-26

Knowing that the Lord is faithful, even when we're not, we can live in hope and not despair. Knowing that the Lord keeps His promises, even when we don't, we can live in hope and not despair. Knowing that the Lord is just and right, even when we're not, we can live in hope and not despair. It is good that a man should both hope and quietly wait for the salvation of the Lord. It is He who will defeat our enemies and lift us out of our distresses. The Lord is the answer to despair. He is the answer to depression. He is the answer to discouragement.

I would seek unto God, and unto God would
I commit my cause: Which doeth great
things and unsearchable; marvellous things
without number: Who giveth rain upon the
earth, and sendeth waters upon the fields:
To set up on high those that be low; that
those which mourn may be exalted to safety.
He disappointeth the devices of the crafty,
so that their hands cannot perform their
enterprise. He taketh the wise in their own

craftiness: and the counsel of the froward is carried headlong. They meet with darkness in the daytime, and grope in the noonday as in the night. But he saveth the poor from the sword, from their mouth, and from the hand of the mighty. So the poor hath hope, and iniquity stoppeth her mouth.

Job 5:8-16

I would seek God and commit to Him my cause so that He can do what He alone can do. So that He can lift me up and set me on high. God is the One who takes us from that lower position of depression and exalts us to a safe place in Him, a place where the enemy cannot exact upon us. It is God who tears down the plans and strategies of the enemy and whose counsel alone will stand. And it is God who saves us from the lies of discouragement, depression, and despair that would put us into the hand of the enemy. And so we have hope. And because we have hope, iniquity must stop her mouth. The mouth of the liar is stopped. Praise God!

Let's get rid of discouragement, depression, and despair by declaring the Word of the Lord. It is only by His grace that we are made free.

"Let the word of Christ dwell in you richly in all wisdom; teaching and admonishing one another in psalms and

*hymns and spiritual songs, singing with grace in your hearts
to the Lord"* (Colossians 3:16).

Wisdom dwells in the Word of Christ, the
anointed word of the living God within us brings us
into wisdom and takes us out of discouragement,
depression, and despair. Wisdom is that which can
elevate us out of the mire of the situation and put us
in a large place. Learning through psalms, hymns,
and spiritual songs lifts us into a place above our
circumstances, where we can receive that wisdom.
Having grace in our hearts is part of the requirement,
and one of the definitions for grace is gratitude.
A heart of thankfulness is a heart that can receive
wisdom. A heart that receives wisdom is a heart free
from discouragement, depression, and despair.

*Father God, I come boldly to You in the name of the
Lord Jesus, and I ask to be delivered from the deception of
witchcraft and its stings of discouragement, depression, and
despair. Remove the veil of darkness that has prevented my
recognition of the subtleties of these spirits and tear down
their stronghold over me, Father.*

*I thank You, Lord, that You are my deliverer, You are
my Messiah, my Redeemer, my risen Lord. I know You are
all-powerful and effective to free me from these spirits and
heal me from their effects in my life. I seek You, Lord, for You
alone do great and marvelous things. You give me the rain of
Your Holy Spirit and wash me in Your living water. You set*

*me on high when I am low and exalt me to a safe place. You
tear down the strategies of the enemy. Because You are my
hope, I have hope.*

*I break all agreement now with discouragement,
depression, and despair. Father, forgive me for entertaining
those spirits and allowing them to stifle the hope in my heart.
I repent to You and declare I will no longer agree with these
evil spirits or give them place in my life. I will change my
thinking. I will focus on You and not myself. I will praise You
continually for Your faithfulness, Your goodness, and Your
might in my life. Thank You for Your sacrifice, Lord Jesus,
which purchased my freedom. Amen.*

The End of the Matter

"Hitherto is the end of the matter. As for me Daniel, my cogitations much troubled me, and my countenance changed in me: but I kept the matter in my heart."

Daniel 7:28

Like Daniel, when God's truth penetrates our hearts, we may feel somewhat troubled. How could we have been so long ignorant of the strategies of the devil? Honestly, it doesn't matter. What matters is what we do with what we now know. How will we respond to God's ability and cleanse ourselves of all perverse speech?

Let this book be a resource to make you aware of who's using your tongue so that you can begin to lend that fiery little member only to the Holy Spirit of the living God. Make your words ever pure and acceptable to God and uplifting to man. Give your heart once

more to Jesus and your words to the advancement of
His kingdom.

Father God, I stand before You just as I am, and I ask
You to forgive me of all my sins. I'm sorry, Lord, for not fully
recognizing Your love for me, for standing afar off from You. I
want to draw near to You today, and I come to the cross, that
the blood of Jesus may touch me. I confess that Jesus Christ
"is come in the flesh," that He died and rose again, that He
is the Son of God and my Redeemer. Wash me in the blood
of Jesus as I declare today that I open my heart and invite
Jesus to come in and reign as my Lord and my Savior. Lord,
I receive Your forgiveness, and I forgive myself. I declare
that from today, I am Your child, and You are my Father. I
dedicate my life to You, Lord. I open my mind and my heart
to Your Word, I give my tongue to the leading of Your Holy
Spirit, and I thank You for my salvation. Amen.

Other Books by
Vicki Smith Berdit
(formerly White)

The Counterfeit Kingdom: ...a False Principality with a Powerless King

Freedom is for Such a Time as Now: Discovering God's Plan for Restoration, and Our Part in It

The Thursday Gift: a Legacy of Jerry White

Yet to be released:

> *Where the River Flows*
>
> *Higher Faith for Greater Power and Deeper Peace*

If this book has blessed you, please contact Freedom's Way Ministries to receive other valuable resources to help you move into your destiny and fulfill your purpose in God. Pastors Phil and Vicki Berdit are available for personal appearances to teach kingdom principles and also for personal ministry.

Permission is given to copy and use the materials in this book for study and teaching to advance the kingdom of God. Donations to Freedom's Way Ministries are gratefully accepted.

Personal ministry is available at no charge. Call 904-993-2876 or go to www.freedomswayministries.com for information.

Notes

1 *Webster's New Universal Unabridged Dictionary.* Second Edition (New York: Simon and Schuster, 1979), s.v. "Disseminate."

2 *Webster's New Universal Unabridged Dictionary.* Second Edition (New York: Simon and Schuster, 1979), s.v. "Rebellion."

3 James Strong, *Strong's Exhaustive Concordance,* s.v. marah, H4784.

4 James Strong, *Strong's Exhaustive Concordance,* s.v. apostasia, G646.

5 James Strong, *Strong's Exhaustive Concordance,* s.v. iqqesh, H6141.

6 James Strong, *Strong's Exhaustive Concordance,* s.v. oudeis, G3762.

7 *Webster's New Universal Unabridged Dictionary.* Second Edition (New York: Simon and Schuster, 1979), s.v. "Dis."

CPSIA information can be obtained
at www.ICGtesting.com
Printed in the USA
FSHW020350201021

9 781637 695708